P9-DGO-221

INSIGHT GUIDES

SYDNEY

Step*by*Step

APA PUBLICATIONS **L**

Part of the Langenscheidt Publishing Group

CONTENTS

ABOUT THIS BOOK

This *Step by Step Guide* has been produced by the editors of Insight Guides, whose books have set the standard for visual travel guides since 1970. With top-quality photography and authoritative recommendations, this guidebook brings you the very best of Sydney in a series of 14 tailor-made tours.

WALKS AND TOURS

The tours in the book provide something to suit all budgets, tastes and trip lengths. As well as covering Sydney's many classic attractions, the routes track lesser-known sights and up-and-coming areas; there are also excursions for those who want to extend their visit outside the city. The tours embrace a range of interests, so whether you are an art fan, a gourmet, a lover of flora and hiking or have kids to entertain, you will find an option to suit.

We recommend that you read the whole of a tour before setting out. This should help you to familiarise yourself with the route and enable you to plan where to stop for refreshments – options for this are shown in the

'Food and Drink' boxes, recognisable by the knife-and-fork sign, on most pages.

For our pick of the walks by theme, consult Recommended Tours For… *(see pp.6–7).*

OVERVIEW

The tours are set in context by this introductory section, giving an overview of the city to set the scene, plus background information on food and drink, shopping, entertainment and outdoor pursuits. A succinct history timeline highlights the key events that have shaped Sydney over the last 240 years.

DIRECTORY

Also supporting the tours is a Directory chapter, comprising a user-friendly, clearly organised A–Z of practical information, our pick of where to stay while you are in Sydney and select restaurant listings; these eateries complement the more low-key cafes and restaurants that feature within the tours and are intended to offer a wider choice for evening dining. Also included here are some nightlife listings.

Above: Sydney sights: beach signs – be careful where you swim; the Australian Museum; Sydney harbour, with its iconic bridge; Bondi lifeguards; the sails of Sydney Opera House, with the bridge behind.

The Author

Ute Junker's career as a travel writer has taken her to many far-flung corners of the globe, but her hometown of Sydney remains one of her favourite places on earth. 'There are few destinations that can match its combination of big-city buzz and spectacular outdoor spaces,' she says. She writes regularly about Sydney for a number of international publications, which has given her an insight into the city's hidden secrets. 'Few of us take the time really to explore the city we live in – I love the fact that my job gives me that opportunity.'

Some of the tours in this book were originally conceived by John Borthwick and David McGonigal.

Margin Tips
Shopping tips, historical facts, handy hints and information on activities help visitors to make the most of their time in Sydney.

Feature Boxes
Notable topics are highlighted in these special boxes.

Key Facts Box
This grey box gives details of the distance covered on the tour, plus an estimate of how long it should take. It also states where the route starts and finishes, and gives key travel information such as which days are best to do the tour or handy transport tips.

Footers
Look here to see the tour name, a map reference and the main attraction on the double-page.

Food and Drink
Recommendations of where to stop for refreshment are given in these boxes. The numbers prior to each restaurant/cafe name link to references in the main text. Restaurants in the Food and Drink boxes are plotted on the individual tour maps.

The $ signs at the end of each entry reflect the approximate cost of a two-course meal for one, with a glass of house wine. Price ranges, which are in Australian dollars and should be seen as a guide only, are also quoted on the inside back flap for easy reference. They are as follows:

$$$$	over A$90
$$$	A$70–90
$$	A$50–70
$	below A$50

Route Map
Detailed cartography shows the tour clearly plotted with numbered dots. For more detailed mapping, see the pull-out map slotted inside the back cover.

ARCHITECTURE

From the rugged sandstone of the city's oldest buildings (tour 1), to the grand residences of former times (tour 5) and the sleek skyscrapers of today (tour 3), Sydney's urban fabric offers diverse delights.

RECOMMENDED TOURS FOR...

ART LOVERS

Explore the shock of the new at the Museum of Contemporary Art (tour 1), take a crash course in Australian art at the Art Gallery of NSW (tour 2) or browse through Paddington's private galleries (tour 6).

CHILDREN

Let the kids run loose among the varied attractions of family-friendly Darling Harbour (tour 4), marvel at the dinosaurs at the Australian Museum (tour 1) or get wet at some of Sydney's best-loved beaches (tour 9).

FLORA AND FAUNA

Get up close and personal with dugongs, sharks and manta rays at the Sydney Aquarium (tour 4), learn about Australia's creepy, crawly and just plain weird fauna at the Australian Museum (tour 1) or keep your eyes peeled for goannas and magpies on the Spit to Manly Walk (tour 11).

FOOD AND DRINK

Sydney is a city of many flavours, so grab some Chinese dumplings (tour 4), savour fish and chips by the harbour (tour 8) or treat yourself to one of its trendy inner-city eateries (tour 5).

GREEN SPACES

Enjoy the diverse charms of the harbourside Royal Botanic Gardens (tour 2), the beaches and bushland of the Royal National Park (tour 14) and the spectacular scenery of the Blue Mountains (tour 13).

HISTORIANS

Get an insight into Australia's earliest days at The Rocks Discovery Museum (tour 1), see how the colony's elite lived at Vaucluse House (tour 7), or learn how Australia was almost discovered by the French at La Perouse and swot up on Captain Cook's landing at Botany Bay (tour 10).

PHOTOGRAPHERS

Wait your turn with the wedding couples at Mrs Macquarie's Chair (tour 2) for the classic Opera House and Harbour Bridge backdrop, shoot back along the length of the harbour from Watsons Bay (tour 8) or get the clifftop perspective from the Bondi to Coogee Walk (tour 9).

SHOPPERS

Discover Sydney's best home-grown fashionistas in the Strand Arcade (tour 1), uncover tomorrow's big names at Paddington Markets (tour 6) or drop by the Object Gallery for the best in Australian craft (tour 5).

SWIMMERS

Savour the silence at secluded Bungan Beach (tour 12), discover your own pocket-sized strip of sand surrounded by bush on the Hermitage Foreshore Walk (tour 7) or swim with the groupers at Clovelly Beach (tour 9).

OVERVIEW

An overview of Sydney's geography, customs and culture, plus illuminating background information on food and drink, shopping, entertainment, outdoor activities and history.

INTRODUCTION

Glitz, the good life and that great blue harbour: this is the image Sydney likes to present to its visitors. Yet this dynamic city is also an economic powerhouse, with a progressive arts scene and close proximity to nature. No wonder Sydneysiders feel they are living in one of the best cities in the world.

Above: Sydney University, Tower and Opera House.

Origin of the Name
Sydney was originally to be called Albion, but Arthur Phillip named it Sydney after the British Home Secretary, Thomas Townshend, Lord Sydney.

Sydney is Australia's first city, in nearly all senses of the word: it was the first European settlement on the continent, proclaimed the first city in 1842; it is the country's largest city, and its pulsing business and financial centre. It is also home to some of the country's most recognisable icons, the Sydney Harbour Bridge, the Sydney Opera House and Bondi Beach.

HISTORY

When you are in the glass-and-concrete heart of the Central Business District (CBD), it is easy to forget how young a city Sydney is. Some 240 years ago, it was little more than a few squalid huts clinging to the edge of the foreshore on The Rocks.

Early Inhabitants, 'Discovery' and First Settlers

Aborigines had inhabited the area for around 45,000 years; the continent was then 'discovered' by Captain Cook in 1770, but it took another 18 years before the first European settlement was created in 1788, with the arrival of the First Fleet under Captain Arthur Phillip.

The first settlers were a motley collection of convicts, and the soldiers sent to guard them. Sydney's early years were grim, with the colony nearly succumbing to starvation in 1790. In 1808, officers of the NSW Corps deposed Governor Bligh in what became known as the Rum Rebellion *(see margin, p.16)*, but it was not until the arrival of Governor Lachlan Macquarie in 1810 that Sydney began the transformation into a colonial capital.

Free Settlers to the Present Day

By 1830, free settlers were arriving in large numbers. The end of transportation in 1840 and the start of the Gold Rush (1851) altered the dynamics of the colony, which had previously functioned more as a military outpost than an urban centre.

Apart from some early structures at The Rocks, many of Sydney's most historic buildings date from Macquarie's time, including the grand buildings along Macquarie Street. His construction programme also included infrastructure such as roads, bridges and wharves, all of which were erected using the convenient convict labour force.

GEOGRAPHY AND LAYOUT

Today's population may be a relatively modest 4.5 million, but Sydney is not by any means a small city. It sprawls across the coastal basin, covering close to 2,000 sq km (1,240 sq miles) with all its suburbs, yet for those who live near the city's compact heart, the most defining feature of its geography is the harbour (actually comprising Port Jackson, which lies between North and South heads, Middle Harbour and North Harbour). The harbour divides the leafy north shore from the urban hub of the south and provides many of the beaches and bays that are Sydneysiders' favourite playgrounds.

Central Sydney

The CBD stretches from the harbour-side district of The Rocks, where Australia's first European colony was founded, south towards Central Station. It's a small area, with narrow Victorian streets that are fairly pedestrian-friendly.

Traffic tends to grind to a standstill within the CBD, and during morning and evening peak hours (7–9am, 5–7pm), the problem extends in all directions. Outside of rush hour, the city's buses and taxis offer a fairly good service, but exploring the city centre – the historic Rocks area, the museums and sights of the CBD and Hyde Park, the Royal Botanic Gardens, Sydney Harbour Bridge and the Sydney Opera House – is easily done on foot. Elsewhere, the inner-city neighbourhoods of Darlinghurst, Surry Hills, Paddington and Woollahra are particularly rewarding areas for a spot of urban strolling amid the pretty Victorian terraces that are typical there.

Close Proximity to Nature

Among the things that set Sydney apart from other world cities are its pockets of untouched nature. Close

Above from far left: looking across the water towards Sydney; enjoying the surf; boomerangs; one of Australia's cuddliest mammals,

Below: arcades on Martin Place.

True Australians

It is estimated that, prior to the arrival of the First Fleet, between 4,000 and 8,000 Aborigines lived in the region. They are commemorated in place names such as Cammeray (after the Cammeraygal tribe) and Ku-ring-gai (after the Gurringgai people).

Above: Sydneysiders.

to the city centre, on the fringes of the harbour foreshore near Rose Bay or Manly, you can find yourself ensconced in a bush landscape that the First Fleeters would recognise. Travel just a little further, to the Royal National Park in the south or the Blue Mountains to the west of the city, and you will find whole landscapes that have remained unaltered for thousands of years.

POPULATION

Like that of many capital cities, Sydney's population is young and diverse. The most striking feature for visitors from Europe and the US may be the city's heavy Asian bias (particularly immigrants from China), though given Australia's geographical location, this should not be too surprising.

Sydney is also known for its large gay and lesbian population, which is particularly visible in the inner-city areas of Darlinghurst and Newtown.

CLIMATE

Sydney's temperate climate is one of its greatest assets, and a boon for travellers. Warm summers (Dec–Feb) are prevented from getting too hot by ocean breezes; in the mild winters (June–Aug), top temperatures rarely drop into single digits; and rain falls only infrequently (although torrid summer downpours do occasionally occur).

The climate's most unpleasant characteristic is a tendency to humidity, particularly in February. Summer is the most popular season for tourists, and while it is a great opportunity to make the most of the city's great outdoors, you may get unpleasantly warm if you are rushing around trying to cram in lots of sights. Spring (Sept–Nov) and Autumn (Mar–May) are very comfortable seasons to be in Sydney.

LOCAL CUSTOMS

The wonderful climate means that Sydneysiders spend a lot of their time outdoors: picnics, swims and barbecues after work are all important. Even when they go to restaurants and bars, alfresco options are a big draw. While Sydney has a big-city buzz, it is also slightly more laidback than many of its global counterparts. While deals aplenty are made in this corporate capital, the city lacks the frenetic vibe of places such as London and New York.

High Standard of Living
Sydneysiders have a passion for living well, which is seen in their dedication to fine dining as well as their penchant for enjoying the water that surrounds the city, whether it be swimming, sailing or simply taking a ride on a ferry. They also take pride in their burgeoning cultural scene, from pocket-sized art galleries to homegrown theatre, to big-name events at

the Sydney Opera House, a symbol of the city's artistic reawakening.

There is a certain brash glamour to Sydney, as there is, for example, in Rio or, to a lesser extent, Los Angeles. With houses, bars and restaurants, it is all about the setting. Without that, the decor had better be sensational.

POLITICS AND ECONOMY

In 2007, the Labor Party won a record fourth term in New South Wales (of which Sydney is the state capital), a result that said more about the disarray among the opposing Coalition forces than about the popularity of Labor. Premier Morris Iemma, who captained the party to its historic win, resigned the next year in the face of disastrous popularity polls; his successor, Nathan Rees, didn't last long, and was quickly replaced by the current incumbent, the former American, Kristina Kenneally.

New South Wales missed out on much of the boom that buoyed the rest of Australia in the early 2000s; and despite boasting the country's financial capital, its economy has trailed the growth rate of other states. How it will fare as a result of the credit crunch remains to be seen, but one thing seems certain: as the Labor government lurches from one crisis to the next, the Coalition seems likely to win the next election.

Above from far left: Sydney Harbour Bridge; view of the city from above.

Below: fireworks over the Sydney Opera House.

FOOD AND DRINK

The secret recipe to Sydney's sensational dining scene? A compelling combination of the world's finest fresh produce (including exceptional seafood), a rich mix of culinary influences from the immigrant population, and a climate that favours alfresco eating.

Fishy Traditions
Sydney's love affair with local seafood – from fish such as snapper and John Dory to crustaceans including blue swimmer crabs and Balmain bugs – is nothing new. Archaeologists investigating Aboriginal middens have found deposits from Sydney rock oyster shells dating to 6,000 BC.

Perhaps the most surprising thing about Sydney's internationally acclaimed restaurant-scene is how recent it is. The first ethnic restaurants opened in the 1950s, and were run by immigrants for immigrants, Australians being highly suspicious of foreigners who did not eat at home like 'respectable folk'.

Once they tried it, however, Sydney-siders loved dining out, and a local cuisine quickly evolved, based on fresh local ingredients and techniques that married European and Asian traditions. 'Modern Australian' cooking is a fusion of the world's great traditional cuisines, particularly French, Italian, Chinese, Japanese, Vietnamese and Thai. The food tends to be fresh, light, low in fat, simply presented and reasonably priced.

'Bush tucker' – traditional plants and meats on which the indigenous Australians survived – makes occasional appearances on menus, with ingredients such as bush tomatoes, lemon myrtle and wattle seeds the most popular. But when Australians talk about 'real Aussie tucker', they probably mean items such as Vegemite (similar to Marmite), meat pies, and desserts such as Lamingtons (sponge cakes) and Pavlovas.

Organic food has yet to make as big an impact as it has in the UK, but it is growing in popularity, with a number of chefs deliberately favouring organic options.

EATING OUT

The dinner rush in Sydney usually starts around 7pm, and, except in a few late-night restaurants, most kitchens close around 10pm. If you are looking for a late-night feed, Chinatown remains your best bet. Tipping is optional; 10 percent is the standard for good service. By law, all restaurants are required to supply diners with tap water free of charge, if requested. Many restaurants close on Mondays.

High-End Restaurants

The undisputed star of Sydney's fine-dining scene is chef Tetsuya Wakada, whose French-Japanese fusion restaurant, Tetsuya's *(see p.115)*, consistently ranks among the world's best. That does not mean he has little competition: the likes of Neil Perry at the Spice Temple *(see p.115)*; Christine Manfield at Universal *(see p.118)*; Guillaume

Brahimi at Guillaume at Bennelong *(see p.116)*; and the Doyle brothers – Greg at Pier and Peter at est. *(see p.114)* – all deliver food that is world-class. Sydney's best restaurants are generally easier to get into than those in London or New York, but you will still need to book ahead, particularly on a Friday or Saturday night.

Casual Dining

While Sydneysiders love a touch of glamour, they are at heart a rather casual breed, which is why the city has an abundance of relaxed eateries. Little distinction is made between brasseries and bistros, pub restaurants and cafés; anywhere that serves up quick and clever meals tends to be popular. Many such places are BYO *(see p.16)*, and most will take reservations.

Ethnic Restaurants

Sydney's hundreds of ethnic restaurants reflect the country's changing immigration patterns. While Italian and Lebanese restaurants remain popular, it is not surprising that Asian restaurants dominate the ethnic dining scene.

Chinatown's dozens of restaurants provide meeting places for the large Chinese community living in nearby high-rise units, with *yum cha*, similar to dim sum in Britain, being particularly popular. There is lots of Japanese cuisine on offer, too, particularly at the ubiquitous sushi bars. However,

Sydneysiders' most passionate long-standing love affair has been with Thai cuisine. Vietnamese cuisine, which shares a similar lightness and freshness, has been catching up recently.

Most ethnic restaurants are simple and unpretentious, but ethnic cuisine has also gone highbrow, with restaurants such as Longrain (Thai, *see p.118*), Billy Kwong (Chinese, *see p.59*) and Ottoman (Turkish; www.ottoman cuisine.com.au) taking it to new levels.

Cheap Eats

Australia has myriad fast-food restaurants – the usual suspects, plus local chains such as Red Rooster for chicken and Hungry Jacks for burgers – but there are many other options for eating on a budget. Cheap ethnic outlets and Asian-style food courts are always popular, but if you are in the mood for

Above from far left: the city is renowned for its superb sea-food; mushy pea pie; the country has a plethora of excellent red and white wines; lamb chops on the barbecue.

Hotel Tradition
Pubs in Australia, whether in towns or outback, were usually called hotels because they also had upstairs rooms that could be rented out.

Farmers' Markets

In the last few years, local farmers' markets have increasingly become the place to buy gourmet produce, from boutique cheese to organic fruit and vegetables. Names to watch out for include Willowbrae cheese, Mandalong lamb and the Jannei goat dairy. The most central markets are the Good Living Growers' Market (Pyrmont Bay Park, opposite Star City Casino, first Sat of the month 7am–11am); Kings Cross Organic Food and Farmers' Market (Fitzroy Gardens, Kings Cross, second and fourth Sat of the month 9am–2pm); The Rocks Farmers' Market (Jack Mundey Place, corner of Argyle and George streets, The Rocks, Fri 10am–3pm).

Rum Rebellion

In 1808, on the 20th anniversary of the founding of the colony, members of the NSW Corps arrested and deposed Governor Bligh in what was Australia's first and only military coup. While rum was important in the early days of the colony as a form of currency – and therefore power – the coup was about much more than just rum, namely the struggle between men wanting to use public authority for their own gain.

something hearty, the two mainstays of budget eating in the suburbs are the local Leagues Club (as in rugby league) and the RSL (Returned Servicemen's League). Both are open to non-members and offer unpretentious meal options and correspondingly good-value drinks. In town, try the NSW Leagues Club (www.nswleagues.com.au), Paddington RSL (www.paddorsl.com.au) or North Bondi RSL (www.northbondirsl.com.au), which also throws stunning views into the mix.

DRINKS

Alcohol has been a key theme in Australian life since the colony's earliest days *(see margin, left)*. Perhaps that is why the authorities have long tried to keep a firm hand on who gets to drink what, and when.

Until the 1950s, Sydney pubs were infamous for the 'six o'clock swill' (the rush for last drinks before the bar closed), and for segregated saloons for men and women. These days, licensing laws have eased considerably, but recent debates about 2am shutouts (when pubs stay open, but no new patrons are allowed in) have once again seen the government seeking to exert more control over the city's drinkers.

Wine

Australian wines are among the world's best, as international wine shows regularly confirm. Sauvignon blanc, Chardonnay and Semillon are the most favoured white varieties, while popular reds include Cabernet Sauvignon, Merlot, Pinot Noir and Shiraz (also known in Europe as Syrah). While areas such as the Hunter Valley, Barossa Valley, Yarra Valley and Margaret River have long enjoyed international reputations, Tasmanian wineries have been getting attention of late, particularly for their Pinot Noir and Riesling.

Many of Sydney's cheaper restaurants are BYO (bring your own). Wine is not sold in most supermarkets, but the city has plenty of bottle shops (off-licences), most of which offer a wide selection at very moderate prices. While Sydney has traditionally lagged behind Melbourne in the wine-bar stakes, the city now boasts a number of very good outlets, including The Winery (285a Crown Street, Surry Hills) and Time To Vino *(see p.123)*.

Wine Tours

The Hunter Valley, famed for its full-bodied Shiraz, fruity Semillon and Chardonnay, lies about two hours from Sydney. Many companies offer day tours to the Hunter for around A$100, including visits to some of the 120 wineries and cellar doors in the district. Try Hunter Valley Wine Tasting Tours (tel: 1800 011 103; www.huntervalleywinetastingtours.com.au) or Boutique Wine Tours (tel: 1800 990 802; www.boutiquewinetours.com.au).

Beer

If there is one thing visitors notice about Australian beer, it is that it is served very cold. Although Foster's lager is the best-known Australian beer internationally, Sydneysiders consider it a beer for tourists, preferring brands such as Tooheys and VB (Victoria Bitter). Some beers are sold in 'new' and 'old' varieties, the first being lager, the latter darker in colour. The alcoholic strength of Australian beer must by law be displayed on the can or bottle. Full-strength draught beer is around 4.9 percent alcohol, 'mid-strength' beer will be around 3.5 percent alcohol, and beers that are marked 'light' will be no more than 2.7 percent alcohol.

Boutique beers, brewed in smaller batches, are popular. Premium commercial brands include Hahn, James Boag and Cascade. Coopers Ale, brewed in South Australia, has a loyal following, and is similar to a British beer but stronger, with 5.8 percent alcohol.

A 285ml (10-ounce) beer glass is called a 'middie' in New South Wales and a 425ml (15-ounce) glass is called a 'schooner'. A small bottle of beer is known throughout Australia as a 'stubbie'. An off-licence is called a bottle shop, or 'bottle-o'. To 'shout' someone a drink means to buy them one, as in, 'Can I shout you a drink?' If someone 'shouts' you, drinking etiquette dictates you should 'shout' them in return.

Cocktails and Spirits

The most famous Australian-made spirit is Bundaberg rum from Queensland, popularly ordered as 'Bundy and Coke'. However, a wide range of spirits is offered in Australian bars, both straight or in cocktails, which in some bars are considered an art form.

Above from far left: Asian-style food is very popular; barbecued shrimps; blackboard menu with local specialities such as Bondi burgers.

Below: sign at a Bondi Beach café.

SHOPPING

From laidback markets to bustling malls and chic boutiques to elegant 19th-century arcades, Sydney has all the retail bases covered. Each neighbourhood has a mix of outlets distinctive to it, and the compact city centre with its department stores and malls offers quick one-stop shopping.

Above: Sportsgirl stripes; foxy bathers; Crocodile Dundee hat.

Bargain-Hunting
Peak sales periods are mid-year (July) and post-Christmas. Boxing Day bargains tend to attract massive crowds, but there are lots of reductions available through to mid-January.

Sydney is a thriving retail centre, with a wide range of local and international products readily available. The city's chief retail precinct and pedestrian area is Pitt Street Mall, which is lined with large shopping centres; elsewhere, smaller boutiques and outlets predominate.

THE ROCKS

The shops along George Street – and the narrow side streets off it – specialise in all kinds of Australiana, from Aboriginal art to opal jewellery to bushman's outfitter R.M. Williams (71 George Street, The Rocks), famed for its riding boots and Akubra hats.

CBD

Sydney's two favourite department stores are a mere two blocks apart, both backing up against Market Street. Myer (436 George Street), the more 'accessible' store, opens onto George Street and Pitt Street Mall, and sells everything from fashion to luggage and homewares. Its more upmarket rival, David Jones, covers

similar ground, but with a more elegant fit-out and higher-end brands; it has two outlets diagonally opposite each other, the Market Street store (nos 65–77) stocking menswear, while the 'Elizabeth Street' store (actually at 86–108 Castlereagh Street) stocks womenswear. Sydney's best food hall is in the basement of the Market Street store.

Castlereagh Street is the place to find international luxury labels, including names such as Louis Vuitton (no. 63), Gucci (MLC Centre) and Chanel (no. 70).

Shopping Centres
Pitt Street Mall is lined with shopping centres, including Westfield, and the nearby Galeries Victoria, which are home to an array of small boutiques and chain stores. The elegant 19th-century Strand Arcade, which also opens onto Pitt Street Mall, houses a quality selection of top designers, while on the other side of George Street, inside another beautiful 19th-century structure, the Queen Victoria Building, you will find many of the chain stores also represented in the Pitt Street Mall.

PADDINGTON

Paddington's leafy backstreets are home to many of the city's most fascinating small galleries, which specialise in Australian, Aboriginal and overseas artists.

Although there are some accessories and homeware shops and bookstores along Oxford Street and side streets such as Glenmore Road and William Street, Paddington's retailers focus heavily on fashion, with home-grown talent mixing it up with chain stores.

SURRY HILLS

Surry Hills is traditionally where young designers open their first store, although some, such as celebrity favourite Wheels and Doll Baby (250 Crown Street), never leave. South Dowling Street and Crown Street are good places to check out fresh talent.

Interiors stores sprout like mushrooms from Campbell to Crown and Bourke streets. Orson & Blake (483 Riley Street) is a favourite with chic young things, while South Dowling Antique Centre (531 South Dowling Street) is a treasure trove of pre-loved goodies.

WOOLLAHRA

If money is no object, look for antiques on Woollahra's leafy Queen Street, where an array of dealers specialise in clocks, jewellery, porcelain, silverware, glassware, books and maps.

Above from far left: jeans at Sass & Bide; Aboriginal art; stylish fashions in Paddington; Bondi logo on a lifeguard-red T-shirt.

Shop Hours
Opening times tend to be 10am to 5pm Monday to Saturday, with shorter hours on Sundays. Thursday is late-night shopping, with many stores open until 9pm.

Sydney's Best Markets

Saturday morning is market time, with each of Sydney's markets having its own vibe. Glebe Market (Glebe Public School, Glebe Point Road; Sat 9.30am–4.30pm) is the hippie market, where tarot card readers and incense stalls mix with quirky handmade clothing, accessories and trinkets. The Rocks Market (George Street; Sat–Sun 10am–5pm) offers one-stop souvenir shopping, with unusual options such as vintage Australian travel posters, wooden fruit bowls made from eucalyptus burls and prints of classic Sydney scenes. Paddington Markets (Paddington Uniting Church, 395 Oxford Street; Sat 10am–4pm) is deservedly Sydney's most famous market, with over 250 different stalls; it is *the* place to catch up-and-coming designers. Paddy's Market (corner of Thomas and Hay streets, Haymarket; Fri–Sun 9am–5pm) is a confusing jumble of cheap and cheerful stalls selling everything from goldfish and toys to underwear, lambskin rugs and fresh fruit and vegetables. Bondi Market (Bondi Beach Public School, Bondi Beach; Sun 10am–4pm) is a mixed bag of beach-side bargains, ranging from vintage clothing and handmade soaps to vinyl records and homewares.

ENTERTAINMENT

From outdoor performances to glamorous harbourside venues, theatres in converted stables to clubs that go on until the small hours, the diversity of Sydney's entertainment scene means there's something for every visitor.

Traditionally, Melbourne has seen itself as the country's custodian of the arts, while Sydney has been painted as more interested in froth than substance. However, Sydney is home to some of the most acclaimed arts companies in the country, such as Company B at Belvoir Street Theatre.

Fretting about the state of the arts is something of an obsession for Australians of a certain class, and it is true that government funding is not always what it could be. The film industry in particular seems to lurch from one crisis to another, while flagship arts companies such as the Sydney Dance Company have had to be bailed out by the government more than once. Despite occasional grim prognoses, however, the companies that do exist often deliver top-quality work.

THEATRE

Sydney's two most high-profile theatre companies have long had distinctly contrasting reputations. The Sydney Theatre Company (STC), with its harbourside home, has traditionally attracted major sponsors, while Company B at Belvoir Street, nestled in an inner-city backstreet, has received less money but more critical acclaim. However, the appointment in 2008 of Cate Blanchett and her playwright husband, Andrew Upton, as co-artistic directors of the STC, is seeing a re-evaluation of that company. Meanwhile, smaller companies such as the Griffin Theatre Company continue to be a crucible for new work. See the Directory *(p.120)* for listings.

DANCE

Australia's dance scene is small, with just three major companies – the Australian Ballet, the Sydney Dance Company and Bangarra Dance Theatre – each committed to showcasing new work. Both the Australian Ballet, under artistic director David McAllister, and Bangarra, under artistic director Stephen Page, enjoy international reputations.

The Sydney Dance Company, by contrast, has had a difficult innings since the departure of founder Graeme Murphy in 2007. It was not until 2009 that a new permanent head – the Spanish choreographer Rafael Moneo – took charge of the company, and it

Summer Screenings
Bondi Pavillion and the park in which it sits is the location of Bondi's Open-Air Cinema, which runs throughout the summer months (www.bondiopenair.com.au). Seated screenings are preceded by local bands and DJs. In town, Centennial Park hosts the Moonlight Cinema (www.moonlight.com.au). There's no seating; unless you hire a beanbag you need to stake out a spot in the grass.

remains to be seen whether he can rejuvenate the company.

MUSIC

Classical Music and Jazz

The Sydney Symphony Orchestra, the city's resident orchestra, welcomed a new artistic director, Vladimir Ashkenazy in January 2009. Like Opera Australia, the orchestra use the Opera House as their Sydney base, leaving the City Recital Hall as the venue of choice for other ensembles such as the Australian Chamber Orchestra and the Brandenburg Orchestra.

Sydney's jazz scene is small but enthusiastic, with The Basement being the most respected venue. For venues, see the Directory *(p.121)*.

Rock and Pop

Australia's popular music scene is alive and well, covering every style from the hard rock of Wolfmother to alternative rockers such as The Living End and Kisschasy and the funky beats of The Presets and the Sneaky Sound System. For listings of the best venues, see the Directory *(p.121)*.

FILM

While actors including Cate Blanchett, Hugh Jackman, Russell Crowe and Nicole Kidman are global stars, Australian directors have fared less well in recent years. While a number, such as

Robert Luketic *(Legally Blonde)* are solidly employed in Hollywood, Baz Luhrman is the only one with name recognition. And while in the 1990s films such as *Mission Impossible 2* and the *Matrix* and *Star Wars* trilogies were filmed here, in recent years Australia has been usurped by cheaper locations such as Canada. For arthouse cinema recommendations, see the Directory *(p.122)*.

NIGHTLIFE

Sydney has no shortage of watering holes and clubs, from small wine bars to pumping clubs. Areas such as King Street Wharf are popular with 20-somethings; the hottest bars are always the latest openings from nightclub king Justin Hemmes. See the Directory *(p.122)* for more recommendations.

Left: on Sydney's small but enthusiastic jazz scene.

Above from far left: the city has thriving theatre and live music scenes.

Above: crowds and a gig at a summer festival in the city.

THE GREAT OUTDOORS

From the beach to the bush, Sydneysiders are spoiled for choice when it comes to getting back to nature. To get a real feel for this aspect of city life, slap on a hat, slop on some sunscreen and head outside.

Sun Protection
Australia has the highest rate of skin cancer in the world, so before you go out, remember to follow the mantra 'slip, slop, slap': slip on a shirt, slop on sunscreen and slap on a hat. If you go out without protection, you will undoubtedly burn.

When the sun shines brightly, Sydneysiders head for the harbour – the blue magnet around which the city has been built – either by sailing on yachts, kayaking or simply walking along the coast. Don't be restricted by this, however, as there are numerous other ways to explore Sydney's most iconic landscapes.

BEACHES

Sydney has over 70 harbour and ocean beaches, most of which are patrolled by volunteer lifesavers. The harbour beaches, such as Balmoral in the north and Nielsen Park in the east, have calm waters and are popular with families. Ocean beaches, such as Bondi and Manly, are popular with surfers and strong swimmers.

Many Sydney ocean beaches are prone to rips or strong currents, so always swim with care. At surf beaches, lifesavers will erect red-and-yellow flags; the zone between the flags is the safe swimming zone. Do not swim outside the flags. If there is a sign saying the beach is closed, do not even think about swimming; lifesavers will not close a beach unless conditions are entirely treacherous. You would be putting your life at risk, as well as theirs.

ISLANDS

The islands of Sydney Harbour form part of the Sydney Harbour National Park, and many of them are open to visitors. The easiest to access is Fort Denison, the tiny fortified outcrop just beyond Circular Quay, from where a regular ferry service to it runs. Daily tours cover the fascinating history of the island, which was used as place of punishment before it was fortified around the time of the Crimean War due to fear of attack from the Russians.

There are also daily services to the largest harbour island, Cockatoo Island, where you can take self-guided tours of various landmarks, including a former shipbuilding site and a convict prison. You can even pitch a tent and overnight on the island.

If all you're after is a picnic on the harbour, Rodd Island, Clark Island and Shark Island are all open to visitors, but Shark Island is the only one served by a regular ferry. For more

information on visiting the harbour islands, contact the Sydney Harbour National Park Information Centre on tel: 02 9247 5033, or www.nationalparks.nsw.gov.au.

NATIONAL PARKS

Sydney is surrounded by a number of national parks that are close enough to be visited on a day trip. To the south, the Royal National Park *(see p.92)* – Australia's oldest – has varied landscapes, from bush to heath, as well as magnificent beaches. However, the Blue Mountains National Park *(see p.84)* remains one of the city's most popular getaways, thanks to its spectacular landscapes and charming towns.

WALKS

You do not have to head out of town to enjoy a good bush walk: Sydney has plenty of pockets of urban bushland that make for a pleasant stroll, as well as some spectacular cliff walks. Three of the best are outlined in detail in this book. The short Hermitage Foreshore Walk *(see p.64)* is an easy, accessible trail, as is the South Head Walk *(see p.66)*. Both these tours enjoy spectacular harbour views. If you like a more challenging trek, the Bondi to Coogee Walk *(see p.70)* is a robust clifftop hike on the oceanside, while the Spit to Manly walk *(see p.78)* takes in magnificent bushland as well as more refined urban surroundings.

Above from far left: pay careful attention to the signs when looking for a place to swim; the leafy Royal National Park; one of the city's many sandy beaches.

Terror of the Deep

With place names such as Shark Island and Shark Point, and several beaches equipped with shark nets, you would be forgiven for wondering what your chances are of encountering Jaws in the waters around Sydney. The short answer is slim. While sharks are regularly spotted in harbour waters, there has not been a fatal shark attack in Sydney harbour since 1963. Popular beaches such as Bondi, Bronte and Tamarama are subject to shark patrols, and if patrollers are concerned about a shark's proximity, they will clear the waters. On the other hand, it is true that shark numbers have been increasing in recent years, due to cleaner waters and more food, and some experts say that it is just a matter of time until the creatures become more invasive. The best advice is to err on the side of caution: do not swim alone, and do not swim in murky waters.

HISTORY: KEY DATES

In the 240 years since the first Europeans arrived, Sydney has seen many dramatic changes: the Aborigines who inhabited the area for thousands of years were close to wiped out, and what started out as a straggling penal settlement has evolved into one of the world's leading cities.

FIRST SETTLEMENT

The First Australians
Thought to have come from Asia and crossed over from New Guinea around 50,000 BC, when there was still a land bridge, Aboriginal Australians settled in the Sydney area around 45,000 BC. They sheltered in harbourside caves, surviving on shellfish, bush food and animals, pursuing a nomadic existence and living in tight territorial groups, with respected elders but no leader.

The Eora people greeted the Europeans calmly at first, but nothing in their experience could prepare them for the future. Before long they had been decimated by massacres and introduced diseases such as smallpox.

AD 1770	Captain James Cook lands at Botany Bay and claims the east coast of Australia for the British Crown.
1778	The First Fleet arrives from England under the command of Captain Arthur Phillip, bringing 736 convicts. A prison camp is set up in Sydney Cove.
1789	The first convict is hanged for murdering a fellow-prisoner. Skirmishes with Aborigines. Smallpox epidemic among Aborigines.
1790	The ill-equipped Second Fleet arrives; the colony nearly succumbs to starvation.
1793	Free settlers arrive in the colony; ex-convict James Ruse sets up the first farm in Parramatta.

COLONIAL CAPITAL

1810	Governor Lachlan Macquarie begins to transform Sydney from a penal settlement to a colonial capital. Ex-forger and architect Francis Greenaway begins designing public buildings.
1815	Explorers Blaxland, Wentworth and Lawson find a route over the Blue Mountains, heralding Sydney's commercial expansion as a port.
1830s	Free settlers begin to arrive in large numbers.
1840	Transportation of convicts to Sydney is abolished.
1850	The University of Sydney is founded.

GOLD-RUSH ERA

1851	Gold is discovered in the Blue Mountains, sparking Australia's first Gold Rush.
1855	The first railway between Sydney and Parramatta opens.

1880	Sydney hosts the southern hemisphere's first world fair.
1900	Bubonic plague results in large areas of Sydney's The Rocks area being razed.

20TH CENTURY

1901	The states join together to become the Commonwealth of Australia. Melbourne is the temporary capital, but Sydney insists that a new capital, Canberra, be built halfway between the two.
1914–18	World War I. Australia suffers high casualties.
1919	Spanish influenza kills more people in Sydney than four years of war.
1932	Sydney Harbour Bridge opens.
1939–45	Sydneysiders enlist again to fight in Europe in World War II.
1942	Troops are withdrawn from Europe, as Japan threatens Australia. Three midget submarines in Sydney Harbour spark panic.
1945	To celebrate the return to peace, the first Sydney to Hobart sailing race is held.
1956	Television comes to Sydney, bringing with it American influences.
1961	The last trams are removed from Sydney's streets. The first sky-scrapers are built in the city.
1971	The first 'green bans' are imposed by the Builders' Labourers Federation to save historic properties from demolition.
1973	Sydney Opera House opens.
1978	The first Gay and Lesbian Mardi Gras parade ends in violence after the police attack participants.
1980	Sydney replaces Melbourne as the financial capital of Australia.
1988	Sydney is the focus of celebrations for Australia's bicentenary. Aborigines campaign for land rights.
1992	Sydney Harbour Tunnel opens.
2000	Sydney hosts a successful Olympic Games.
2006	Sydney is covered in smoke after raging fires in the Blue Mountains.
2007	The Labor Party is re-elected to NSW (New South Wales) gov-ernment for a historic fourth term.
2008	The Federal government apologises to Aborigines for past wrongs.
2010	Deputy Prime Minister Julia Gillard deposes Kevin Rudd to become Australia's first female prime minister. After an election results in a hung parliament, she enlists the support of independent MPs to form a government.

Above from far left:
Captain Cook's ship *The Endeavour* aground on the Great Barrier Reef, by William Byrne (1743–1805); building the Sydney Harbour Bridge, which opened in 1932.

News and Views
Australia's first broadsheet news-paper, *The Sydney Gazette*, was first published in Sydney in 1803. Today, Australia's two biggest publishers, Fairfax Media and News Ltd, are both based in Sydney.

WALKS AND TOURS

CITY CENTRE HIGHLIGHTS

This tour takes you through 240 years of Sydney's history, from The Rocks – where the fledgling colony began – to the 21st-century heart of the Central Business District (CBD), with the chance to do a bit of shopping thrown in.

Above: The Rocks Market; quirkily dressed street entertainer; Museum of Contemporary Art.

Original Road
George Street is the oldest European road on the Australian continent, and can be seen on maps dating back as far as 1791.

DISTANCE 7km (4½ miles)
TIME A full day
START Sydney Visitor Centre
END Australian Museum
POINTS TO NOTE
This tour is best done at the weekend if you want to catch The Rocks Market in full swing. The distance noted above is for the route drawn in red on the map but doesn't include the bus trip in between.

One of Sydney's main tourist areas, The Rocks is buzzing by day, alive with people wandering around its shops, sights, cafes, pubs and restaurants. To the south, the Central Business District (CBD) includes soaring buildings, Victorian landmarks and Hyde Park.

THE ROCKS

To the west of Circular Quay is the area known as The Rocks, a sandstone peninsula, where the First Fleet stumbled ashore after its eight-month voyage, and set about building a colony.

Originally, it comprised a ragged jumble of wharves and warehouses, hovels, brothels, pubs and shops; by the late 19th century, it had become a slum of seedy houses and pubs. An outbreak of bubonic plague early in the 1900s led to a government clean-up and the demolition of the worst of the buildings.

Another spate of demolition occurred in the 1920s, to make room for the approaches to the Harbour Bridge, which opened in 1932. In the 1960s, it was proposed to level the area entirely to make way for a mini-Manhattan; the plan was defeated when residents enlisted the support of building unions, who placed 'green bans' on the work, and since the 1970s the stress here has been on preservation and renovation.

Sydney Visitor Centre

West of Circular Quay is the starting point of this tour, the **Sydney Visitor Centre ❶** (corner of Argyle and Playfair streets; tel: 1800 067 676; www.shfa.nsw.gov.au; daily 9.30am–5.30pm). The staff are very helpful, and you can stock up here on brochures and maps.

The Rocks Discovery Museum

Go downstairs, walk to the far end of the building and exit to the right to find **The Rocks Discovery Museum** ❷ (Kendall Lane; tel: 02 9240 8680; www.therocks.com.au; daily 10am–5pm; free). This small museum provides an excellent introduction to the area's indigenous inhabitants, the early days of the colony, and how it has evolved.

If you can, look out of the back door of the museum to peep at the tiny backyards and courtyards of the kind that once predominated in this part of town.

The Rocks Market

Turn right out of the front of the museum on to Kendall Lane and follow this road on to George Street, where you should turn left to hit **The Rocks Market** ❸ (George and Playfair streets; tel: 02 9240 8717; www.therocks.com.au; Sat–Sun 10am–5pm),

Above from far left: Queen Victoria Building; Sydney's Central Business District (CBD) from above; George Street.

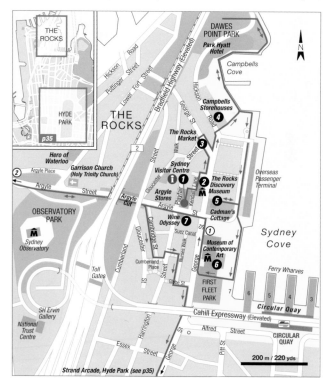

Watering Holes

If you have walked up a thirst, The Rocks' many pubs include some of Sydney's oldest. Aside from the Lord Nelson (*see opposite*), try the Fortune of War Hotel (137 George Street; tel: 02 9247 2714): beer has been served on this site since 1839. An alternative is the Hero of Waterloo (81 Lower Fort Street; tel: 02 9252 4553), where the cellars were reportedly used as holding cells for press-ganged sailors.

although note that this is open at weekends only. It comprises lots of stalls, selling wares from jewellery to craft items such as fruit bowls carved from native hardwoods.

Campbells Cove

After spending time at the market, pick up Hickson Road briefly, then turn right, down to the water. To your left are the impressive **Campbells Storehouses ➍**, named after trader Robert Campbell, who built them in 1838. These days they house a number of restaurants.

Follow the path north along the water, past the five-star Park Hyatt Hotel, which has some of the best views in Sydney, to the pretty park on **Dawes Point**, a scenic spot that is popular for wedding photos.

Observatory Hill

Observatory Hill, off Argyle Street, is the highest natural point in the city, and has at various times housed a windmill (1796), then a half-built fort (1803) and a shipping signal station (1848). Today it is home to two notable museums: the Sydney Observatory (Watsons Road, Observatory Hill; tel: 02 9921 3485; www.sydneyobservatory.com.au; daily 10am–5pm and evenings Apr–Mar; charge), which has a 3-D space theatre and a planetarium, as well as some impressive telescopes; and the S.H. Ervin Gallery. Housed within the National Trust Centre, the gallery (Watsons Road, Observatory Hill; tel: 02 9258 0173; www.nationaltrust.com.au; Tue–Sun 11am–5pm; charge) has a very good collection of Australian figurative art.

Cadman's Cottage

Retracing your steps, follow the waterfront back towards Circular Quay. After you pass the high-end restaurants housed in the Overseas Passenger Terminal on your right you will come to **Cadman's Cottage ➎** (110 George Street; tel: 02 9247 5033; Tue–Sun 10am–4.30pm; free), the oldest residence in central Sydney, and the only one that gives a feel for the simple constructions of the colony's early days. It was built in 1816 to house the governor's coxswain and crew, and is named after John Cadman, the last coxswain to live there. The building originally fronted onto a sandy beach, but, due to land reclamation, is now set well back from the water.

Museum of Contemporary Art

Just past Cadman's Cottage, on your right is the massive Art Deco bulk of the **Museum of Contemporary Art ➏** (140 George Street; tel: 02 9245 2400; www.mca.com.au; daily 10am–5pm; free). The museum has a permanent collection of Australian, modern Aboriginal and international art and hosts a variety of excellent temporary exhibitions. It also has a good gift shop.

By now you probably be in need of refreshment, and there are a large number of options on George Street. Some 50m/yds north of the museum some of the best Thai food in Sydney can be sampled at the stylish **Sailor's Thai** eatery, see ⑪①.

Wine Odyssey

For more liquid refreshment, cross George Street, take the first left at Argyle Street and opposite the Visitor Centre is **Wine Odyssey** ❼ (corner of Harrington and Argyle streets; tel: 1300 136 498; www.wine odyssey.com.au; Sun–Wed noon–10pm, Thur–Sat noon–midnight; charge). This wine bar and education centre brings some of Australia's lesser-known wines to a broader audience. On offer are tastings of 50 hand-picked wines that are usually only available to the public at the winery itself. In the Aroma Room you can take in 50 wine smells, while in the Tasting Theatre you can learn about six of Australia's best niche wineries. The shop sells more than 400 wines by the bottle, and there is also an a la carte restaurant.

Argyle Cut

If beer is more your scene, take a detour and head west up Argyle Street through the Argyle Cut, a massive tunnel carved out by convicts. As you emerge, the **Garrison Church** is on your right and **Observatory Hill** *(see feature box, opposite)* to your left. Continue west for another block and you will reach the **Lord Nelson Brewery Hotel**, see ⑪②. This atmospheric sandstone hotel is one of the oldest pubs in The Rocks *(see margin, left)* and still brews its own beer on site.

Nurses Walk

Head back down the Argyle Cut and

Above from far left: Cadman's Cottage; pulling a pint in the historic Lord Nelson.

Above: exterior of the Lord Nelson and portrait of the distinguished seafarer himself.

Food and Drink 🍽

① SAILOR'S THAI AND SAILOR'S THAI CANTEEN

106 George Street, The Rocks; tel: 02 9251 2466; www.sailorsthai.com.au; Mon–Sat L, D; $$–$$$

There are two options here to suit different budgets, both of which deliver sensational Thai. At street level is the lower-priced option, a canteen with a communal table and open kitchen in the newer part of the building; downstairs the restaurant is housed in an old sandstone sailors' home on the waterfront, and is an atmospheric place for a weekday lunch or dinner.

② LORD NELSON BREWERY HOTEL

19 Kent Street, The Rocks; tel: 02 9251 4044; www.lordnelsonbrewery. com.au; bar: Mon–Sat L, D, Sun Br, L, D; brasserie: Thur–Fri L, D, Tue–Wed and Sat D; $$

One of The Rocks' true treasures, this sandstone pub has been serving beer since 1831, although the current name dates back to 1841. Try one of the six beers brewed on site along with some pub fare, or enjoy quality dining in Nelson's Brasserie upstairs.

Prepay Buses
All the buses along George Street are now prepay only, so if you need a ticket, you have to buy one from newsagents and other shops marked with a bus tickets sign.

take the first turning on your right, Cambridge Street, which will lead you into a warren of narrow, atmospheric streets that were once typical of the area. Follow the signs for the Mission Stairs to Nurses Walk, then turn right, and walk 50m/yds before turning left into George Street.

CBD

From here, hop on any of the buses heading south along George Street (noting the margin tip, *see left*) and ask to be let out at the Strand Arcade in the heart of the Central Business District (CBD).

Strand Arcade

The **Strand Arcade** ❽ (412 George Street; tel: 02 9232 4199; www.strand arcade.com.au) is one of Sydney's architectural gems, with tiered mezzanines and decorative ironwork. Connecting George and Pitt streets, it houses a variety of boutiques on the first and second floors (check out local designers such as Little Joe by Gail Elliot, Jayson Brunsdon, Leona Edmiston and Alannah Hill), as well as a collection of appealing cafes, including **Pendolino**, see ❦③.

Sydney Tower

Walk through the Strand Arcade and emerge on to the Pitt Street Mall, Sydney's pedestrian shopping zone. Head south and enter the Westfield shopping centre (partly closed until 2012) on your left for the **Sydney Tower** ❾ (Podium Level; tel: 02 9333 9222; www.sydney tower.com.au; daily 9am–10.30pm; charge), the tallest building in Sydney.

From the observation deck 250m (820ft) above street level, you can enjoy 360-degree views of the city, or, if you like an adrenalin rush, buy a Skywalk ticket to traverse the outdoor walkways and glass-floor overhangs at the top of the tower. Your ticket includes a seat in the 3-D *OzTrek* show, a trip through Australia's cultural history and geography, taking in everything from white-water rafting down a tropical Queensland river to a close encounter with a saltwater crocodile.

Queen Victoria Building

Exit on Pitt Street and walk west down Market Street for one block to reach the **Queen Victoria Building** ❿ (QVB; 455 George Street; tel: 02 9264 9209; www.qvb.com.au; Mon–Wed and Fri–Sat 9am–6pm, Thur 9am–9pm, Sun 11am–5pm), which occupies an entire block of George Street between

---

Food and Drink

③ **PENDOLINO**
Level 2, Strand Arcade, George Street, Sydney; tel: 02 9231 6117; www.penolino.com.au; Mon–Sat L, D
This sexy space at the top of the Strand Arcade is the place to come for fabulous regional Italian cuisine. If you're not in the mood for a meal, the adjacent café offers delicious breakfasts, before reinventing itself as a wine bar in the evening.

Market and Druitt streets. Built in 1898 to celebrate Queen Victoria's golden jubilee, the building, which once housed tradespeople, showrooms and a concert hall, was built on the site of a street market and fell into neglect before being entirely refurbished in 1986 as a three-storey shopping arcade. A second (A$35.5 million) refurbishment, completed in 2009, has enhanced its exquisite 19th-century interiors, which include leadlight wheel windows and original floor tiles.

Sydney Town Hall

Emerging at the Druitt Street end of the QVB, cross Druitt Street to come to **Sydney Town Hall ⓫** (483 George Street; tel: 02 9265 9189; Mon–Fri 9am–6pm; free), a sandstone building in the Victorian style. Interior highlights include the stunning Vestibule Room, which features magnificent stained glass and a massive crystal chandelier, and the Centennial Hall, dominated by the largest tubular-pneumatic organ ever built, with around 8,700 pipes. Free organ recitals are held regularly.

HYDE PARK

Head east up Park Street (the extension of Druitt Street) for three blocks and you will reach **Hyde Park ⓬** on Elizabeth Street. Named after London's famous green space, it was originally used as a racecourse but is now divided into two halves by Park

Above from far left:
Strand Arcade;
Queen Victoria
Building; Sydney
favourite, the
Archibald Fountain,
in Hyde Park.

Below: Art Deco
ANZAC Memorial (see
p.34) in Hyde Park.

Archibald Fountain
Hyde Park's Archibald Fountain, a neo-classical bronze-and-granite design by French sculptor François Sicard, commemorates the alliance of Australian and French forces in World War I.

Street. An impressive boulevard of trees runs through the centre of its northern end, opening onto the 1932 **Archibald Fountain** *(see left)*. Just near the corner of Park and College streets, in the sunken Sandringham Memorial Gardens, is a pergola that becomes a cascade of flowering wisteria in September.

At the south end of the park, the Art Deco **ANZAC Memorial and Pool of Remembrance** ⑬ (tel: 02 9267 7668; www.anzacmemorial.nsw. gov.au; daily 9am–5pm; free) was erected in 1934 to commemorate the troops from New South Wales who served in World War I.

AUSTRALIAN MUSEUM

Head back up to Park Street and turn east: opposite the south end of Hyde Park is the **Australian Museum** ⑭ (6 College Street; tel: 02 9320 6000; www.australianmuseum.net.au; daily 9.30am–5pm; charge). Established in 1827, it is Australia's oldest museum and enjoys an international reputation in the fields of natural history and indigenous research. It's a great place to learn about Australia's unique flora, fauna and cultures.

Dinosaurs

Start on the top floor of the three-storey building, where two of the most popular exhibits are found. The Dinosaurs exhibit is a favourite with kids of all ages, with the highlights being the 10 complete skeletons and eight life-size models. Some of Australia's distinctive dinosaurs are on display, including **Eric the Pliosaur**. Found in the opal-mining town of Coober Pedy, Eric is unique in that during the fossilisation process, his entire skeleton was replaced with opal.

Australian Fauna

On the same floor is **Surviving Australia**, a fabulous exhibition devoted to Australia's unique fauna, from Tasmanian devils and platypuses to deadly spiders and snakes (the 10 most venomous snakes in the world are all found in Australia). The exhibit is divided into sections dealing with separate habitats, including a section on the animals that can be found in both urban and suburban environments. Also enthralling is the exhibit devoted to extinct fauna, including six species of marsupial lion, which weighed up to 160kg (350lbs).

Skeletons and Minerals

If you have under-5s with you, duck into **Kidspace**, where children can get hands-on with artefacts as well as playing with puzzles, puppets and dressing-up clothes. Alternatively, head down to the first floor to inspect a dazzling collection (one of the world's best) of multicoloured minerals, before continuing down to the ground floor where the skeleton gallery fascinates

visitors of all ages. Favourite exhibits include Jumbo the elephant and the Bone Ranger, a human skeleton sitting on a skeletal horse.

Indigenous Australians

Also on this floor is the museum's other key attraction, a fascinating section devoted to Indigenous Australians, and featuring 40,000 different exhibits representing the diverse experience of Aborigines and Torres Strait Islanders. This culture, which included around 700 languages, flourished for over 40,000 years before the Europeans arrived. Learn about The Dreaming, which forms the basis of much of Aboriginal spirituality, and examine Aboriginal art that has attracted international interest in recent decades.

Historical events and politics are also addressed, including the 1960s Freedom Rides – inspired by the US Civil Rights Movement – and the Stolen Generations. Between the late 1800s and the 1970s, some 100,000 indigenous children were taken from their families and placed in white homes or institutions – behaviour that shocked Australia when it became the subject of a national inquiry in 1997. In 2000, 250,000 people marched across the Sydney Harbour Bridge to call for reconciliation and a national apology, which did not come until February 2008, when new Prime Minister Kevin Rudd made it one of his first official acts.

Ending the Tour

To finish off a long day, walk back across the park to Elizabeth Street and enjoy a quiet drink in one of the city's nicest wine bars, **Bambini Trust Wine Room**, see ⑪④.

Above from far left: Aboriginal art, dinosaur skeleton and exterior, all at the Australian Museum.

Food and Drink

④ BAMBINI TRUST WINE ROOM
185 Elizabeth Street; tel: 02 9283 7098; www.bambini trust.com.au; Mon–Sat D; $$
This exquisite little Parisian-style bar has an extensive list of wines by the glass, including European options and a diverse Australian selection. Nibbles include whisky-cured salmon gravlax with remoulade and rye. For a more substantial meal, book at the classy restaurant.

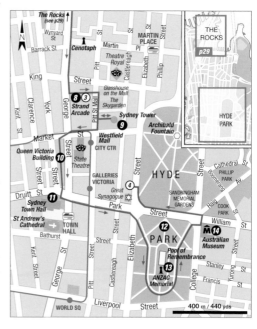

HARBOUR HIGHLIGHTS

Sydney's two great icons, the Harbour Bridge and the Opera House, kick off this walk, which then takes in nearby foreshore must-sees on the south side, including the Royal Botanic Gardens.

DISTANCE 8km (5 miles)
TIME A full day
START Sydney Harbour Bridge
END Woolloomooloo
POINTS TO NOTE
If it is a nice day, pack your swimming costume: you can take a dip either before commencing the walk in North Sydney *(see margin, right)* or at the Andrew (Boy) Charlton Pool *(see p.40).*

Climbing Sydney Harbour Bridge

For over 10 years Bridgeclimb has organised three-and-a-half-hour tours of the bridge, culminating at the apex of the arch, 134m (440ft) above sea level. Tours are available during the day and night, and at sunset and sunrise. For more information, contact Bridgeclimb (tel: 02 8274 7777; www.bridgeclimb.com).

Right: tackling the bridge's many steps.

The harbour is very much a focal point for the city, and this walk takes in the best of the central foreshore. Starting on the North Shore, it crosses the Harbour Bridge, wends its way to the Opera House and through the Royal Botanic Gardens to the Art Gallery of NSW, finishing in the former working-class enclave of Woolloomooloo.

SYDNEY HARBOUR BRIDGE

It is hard to imagine the city without the celebrated **Sydney Harbour Bridge ❶**, which opened in 1932 and was for a long time the world's largest single-span bridge. Before it was opened, up to 40 million passengers a year crossed the water by ferry. These days, the bridge is supplemented by a tunnel, which still has heavy flows in peak hour. The A$20 million bridge took 1,400 workers nine years to construct, and cost 16 of them their lives. It has eight lanes, two rail lines, a footpath and a cycle path.

The opening ceremony was famously disrupted when, as a political statement against the socialist goverment of the time, Francis de Groot galloped forward on his horse and slashed the ribbon with his sword, declaring the bridge open 'in

the name of the decent citizens of New South Wales'. De Groot was removed, the ribbon tied back together, and the ceremony continued.

There are four ways to cross the bridge: drive, take the train, cycle or walk. If you want to walk (about a 30-minute stroll), catch the train to Milson's Point station and exit to the east to climb the sandstone stairs that lead to the footpath that runs the span of the bridge. If you feel like tackling the 200 steps to the top of the south-eastern pylon, you will find a museum on the bridge's history and a viewing platform. Tours of the bridge are also offered *(see margin, left)*.

CIRCULAR QUAY

At the southern end of the bridge are stairs down to The Rocks *(see p.28)*, but to continue this tour walk up another flight of steps and continue on

Above from far left: Sydney Harbour Bridge; the Opera House from above.

Milson's Point

Two of the North Shore's favourite attractions lie a short walk from Milson's Point station. North Sydney Olympic Swimming Pool (4 Alfred Street South; tel: 02 9955 2309; Mon–Fri 5.30am–9pm, Sat–Sun 7am–7pm; charge) has one of the best locations in Sydney, directly on the water under the Harbour Bridge. Indoor and outdoor pools make it worth visiting the entire year. Next door is Sydney's favourite and oldest amusement park, Luna Park (tel: 02 9922 6644; www.lunaparksydney.com; free entry, charge for rides only).

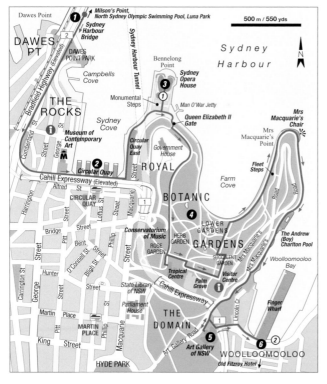

Bennelong Point
The Eora called the site of the Opera House, Tjubagali. It was a place of celebration even then and a large midden site of white cockleshells (the name means 'white mud clay'), which also has a curious parallel with the modern-day structure.

Below: close up of the Opera House, showing its scaly sails.

the walkway that runs alongside the Cahill Expressway. After 10–15 minutes, you will come to a lift that takes you down to **Circular Quay ❷**, which is always crowded with a mix of commuters and tourists, entertained by buskers. Large plaques along the quay are part of a Writers Walk honouring famous Australian authors, giving details of their careers and works.

Walk east along the quay towards Bennelong Point and the Opera House. East Circular Quay – a mix of residences, boutiques, restaurants and bars – was developed in the run-up to the millennium, and was at first hugely controversial. When the 1960s office blocks that had stood on the site were torn down, Sydneysiders got used to the open space and protested strongly when the apartment building known as The Toaster was developed. However, it has now become part of the city fabric.

SYDNEY OPERA HOUSE

Next on the tour is the iconic **Sydney Opera House ❸** (Bennelong Point; tel: 02 9250 1777; www.sydneyopera house.com; free), designed by Danish architect Jørn Utzon. Finished in 1973, the controversial build took 14 years to complete and was fraught with problems, but today it is the city's most popular building.

In addition to operas and symphony concerts, the building hosts drama, comedy, contemporary music and experimental performances *(see p.121)*, with events regularly held on the forecourt, where the stone stairs double up as seating.

Spectacular Design
The design's most striking features are the sail-like structures, suggestive of yachts on the harbour; these are covered with a million anti-fungal tiles and weigh 158,000 tonnes. A number of engineering and financial problems forced the government to scale the project down from Utzon's original

vision, leading the architect to resign in protest. Nevertheless, the original A$7 million budget topped A$102 million by the time the building was completed, much of which came from government lotteries.

Concerts and Performances

The Queen opened the Opera House in 1973. The first production in the intimate Opera Theatre was Prokofiev's *War and Peace*, while in the Concert Hall it was Beethoven's Ninth Symphony. Today, more than 3,000 performances and events are held here annually. The Opera House has several restaurants, including a fine dining option, **Guillaume at Bennelong** *(see p.116)*, the casual **Mozart Café** and the popular **Opera Bar**, see ⑪①.

ROYAL BOTANIC GARDENS

At the foot of the Monumental Steps at the front of the Opera House, turn left and walk 100m/yds to the Queen Elizabeth II Gate, which takes you into the **Royal Botanic Gardens** ④

(tel: 02 9231 8111; www.rbgsyd.nsw. gov.au; daily 7am–sunset; free). The gardens' 30 hectares (74 acres) loop around Farm Cove, or Woccanmagully ('crow headland'), as the Aborigines called it. The colony's first farm and the governor's kitchen garden became the Botanic Gardens in 1816. Governor Macquarie appointed Charles Fraser, a soldier, as the first colonial botanist. Explore the gardens by taking the trackless train (with commentary), which tours at regular intervals, or spend a pleasant hour or so simply wandering through them as explained below.

Herbs and Roses

Start by heading south up to the **Herb Garden**, just behind the **Conservatorium of Music** *(see p.46)*, where there are displays charting the history of herbs. In the nearby **Rose Garden**, the plantings chart the history and diversity of the rose. Keep heading south to come to the magnificent **Tropical Centre**, where you can walk through two modern glasshouses where humidity is kept at a minimum of 75

Above from far left: Sydney Opera House and Harbour Bridge from above; cacti in the Royal Botanic Gardens.

Harbour Trips and Taronga Zoo
No visitor to Sydney should miss out on a ferry trip around the harbour, and, if time allows, a boat trip across to Taronga Zoo. Located on a picturesque headland, the zoo offers spectacular views across the harbour, as well as the chance to come face-to-face with Australian animals including koalas and kangaroos, platypus, echidnas and wombats.

Food and Drink

① OPERA BAR
Lower Concourse Level, Opera House, Bennelong Point; tel: 02 9247 1666; www.operabar.com.au; daily L, D; $$
Guillaume *(see p.116)* at Bennelong, the Opera House's fine-dining venue, is an experience, but not one that everyone can afford, so for those looking for a great Sydney experience at a cheaper price, the indoor-outdoor Opera Bar is the place to go. During the day, the vibe is relaxed; at night, it is positively buzzing, with DJs spinning great tunes.

Above from left:
admiring the displays
in the Art Gallery
of South Wales;
the waterfront
in Woolloomooloo.

Summer Fun
In January The
Domain is the venue
for a number of free
outdoor concerts,
including Jazz in The
Domain, Symphony
in The Domain and
Opera in The Domain.
For more information,
visit www.sydney
festival.org.au.

percent. The **Pyramid** contains native Australian tropical species, while the **Arc** displays exotic tropical species.

Palm Grove

To the east of the glasshouses lies the **Palm Grove**, which dates back to the 19th century and contains nearly 150 species. Nearby is the **RBG Shop and Visitor Centre** (tel: 9231 8125; daily 9.30am–5pm), opposite which lies a stunning **Succulent Garden** featuring cacti and other species from the deserts of South Africa and the Americas.

The Lower Gardens

Keep heading north to enter the Lower Gardens, 5 hectares (12 acres) of reclaimed land, landscaped in typical 19th-century style, complete with formal plantings, framed vistas, ornate statues and a series of picturesque little ponds created by the damming of a small creek.

Follow the sea wall heading east and you will come to the **Fleet Steps**, built for the benefit of sailors disembarking from ships at Farm Cove. During January and February, the ever-popular St George Open-Air Cinema is held here.

Further along is one of Sydney's most popular spots for wedding photos, **Mrs Macquarie's Chair**, a ledge that was carved from sandstone to enable Governor Macquarie's wife to sit comfortably while admiring one of the most magnificent harbour views in the world.

Keep following the foreshore path to come to another of Sydney's waterside swimming pools. The **Andrew (Boy) Charlton Pool** (1c Mrs Macquarie's Road; tel: 02 9358 6686; www.abcpool. org; charge) is named after a swimming champion of the 1920s and 1930s, and has a cafe. Further along the road leads up to The Domain (see margin, left), the 30-hectare (72-acre) spread of open parkland abutting the Botanic Gardens to the south and east. Opposite lies the Art Gallery of NSW.

ART GALLERY OF NEW SOUTH WALES (NSW)

Fronted by an imposing 1909 neo-classical facade with a huge portico, the **Art Gallery of NSW** ❺ (Art Gallery Road, The Domain; tel: 02 9225 1700; www.artgallery.nsw.gov.au; Thur–Tue 10am–5pm, Wed 10am–9pm; free) is one of the country's best galleries, holding significant collections of Australian, Asian and European art, in addition to hosting special exhibitions and events (talks, films and music, etc).

Food and Drink 🍴

② **HARRY'S CAFE DE WHEELS**
Cowper Wharf Road, Woolloomooloo; tel: 02 9211 2506;
www.harryscafedewheels.com.au; daily L, D; $
Harry's is a Sydney institution. For over 60 years, a peas-and-mash pie (now called 'The Tiger') has been the favourite way to finish up a big night. Even during the day you will often see punters queuing to sink their teeth into one of Harry's finest.

This is a good place to get an overview of Australian art, with artists such as Arthur Boyd, Sidney Nolan, Grace Cossington-Smith, John Olsen and Brett Whiteley *(see p.58)* being well represented. On the third level, the **Yiribana Gallery** has an outstanding collection of traditional and contemporary Aboriginal and Torres Strait Islander work. Started in the 1950s, it is now one of the largest collections of indigenous art in the world and includes a fine collection of bark paintings.

Also worth visiting is the ground-floor **Asian Gallery**, where artworks from across the region – with a particular emphasis on Japanese and Chinese art – are displayed.

WOOLLOOMOOLOO

Leaving the gallery, turn right to find the steps leading down to **Wool-loomooloo** ❻. Long one of the city's grittiest areas and still home to a large amount of public housing, the district's gentrification only started in the 1990s when the 400m/yd-long Finger Wharf was redeveloped into apartments, a private marina, a string of stylish waterside restaurants and a hotel. Stop here for a refreshment, or try one of the old-school pubs opposite *(see margin, right)*. Alternatively, chow down at the well-loved **Harry's Cafe de Wheels**, see ⑪②, which has been selling pies since 1945.

Old Fitzroy Hotel
As befits a working-class suburb, Woolloomooloo has more than its fair share of pubs, but perhaps the best value is the Old Fitzroy Hotel, which has its own studio theatre hosting a range of fringe productions. The combined beer, laksa and theatre ticket offers Sydney's best-value night out (129 Dowling Street; tel: 02 9356 3848; www. oldfitzroy.com.au).

The Harbour Islands

Sydney has several harbour islands, some of which are open to visitors. The most notorious is Fort Denison, which gained its nickname 'Pinchgut' from its days as a place of punishment. The island and its small fort are open daily for visitors, and host regular tastings of Australian wine and cheese (www.mcintoshandbowman.com). Ferries depart from Circular Quay. Goat Island (open for special events only) – one of the largest – has convict-era architecture and historic port facilities, and is an occasional venue for concerts. Rodd, Clark and Shark islands make great picnic spots and are open every day from 9am to sunset. A regular ferry service runs from the harbour to Shark Island; to visit Clark or Rodd islands, you will need to organise your own transport. For more information on visiting the harbour islands, contact Sydney Harbour National Park Information Centre (tel: 02 9247 5033; www.nationalparks.nsw.gov.au).

3

THE CBD AND WALSH BAY

This tour is one for architecture buffs, taking in the highlights of the Central Business District (CBD), where Sydney's mini-Manhattan skyline is studded with statement buildings by internationally acclaimed architects. Also here are older gems from the Colonial and Victorian periods. Nearby is Walsh Bay.

Tallest Tower
For the past 30 years, Sydney's skyline has been dominated by Sydney Tower *(see p.32)*, known to locals as Centrepoint Tower. At 303m (990ft) it is the city's highest structure. As late as the 1960s, that honour was held by the AMP building at Circular Quay, which is now dwarfed by all its neighbours.

DISTANCE 7km (4½ miles)
TIME A half-day
START St Mary's Cathedral
END 30 The Bond
POINTS TO NOTE
St Mary's Cathedral is located on the eastern side of Hyde Park. Start this tour in the afternoon and aim to finish in the evening, when the theatre district comes alive and you can savour a glass of wine and a snack in one of the area's waterside bars.

Two hundred years of history are revealed in the streetscapes of Sydney's Central Business District (CBD), where the ongoing battle between preservation and progress has resulted in buildings from different decades and different centuries nestling cheek by jowl.

An Architectural History

The city's most homogeneous architectural zones are the adjoining areas of Macquarie Street and Martin Place, which serve as an interesting illustration of the colony's changing ambitions. The early government buildings lining Macquarie Street are relatively modest sandstone constructions: less than 100 years later, a growing self-confidence led to the far more grandiose Victorian visions planted on Martin Place by capitalists grown rich on exporting commodities such as wool.

Although the building boom of the 1960s and 1970s destroyed many of the city's historic buildings, a lot of the survivors, such as Customs House and the former GPO, have been restored recently. The city's silhouette continues to evolve, most recently with new buildings by internationally acclaimed architects such as Renzo Piano, and industrial conversions such as the wharves along Hickson Road.

ST MARY'S CATHEDRAL

There's something peculiarly Australian about the conjunction of **St Mary's Cathedral ❶** (corner of Col-

lege and Cathedral streets; tel: 02 9220 0400; www.stmaryscathedral.org.au; Mon–Fri 7am–6pm, Sat 8.30am–7pm, Sun 7am–7pm; charge for crypt only), the city's most significant Catholic cathedral, and the construction erected facing it across a plaza: an indoor swimming pool. This doesn't, however, detract from the building, and St Mary's remains one of the city's most impressive Victorian buildings.

Designed by an Anglican, William Wardell, in Gothic style, its generous proportions are much larger than many of the European classics that inspired it, with the vaulted roof reaching up 46m (150ft) high.

The cathedral was opened in 1885, although it was not entirely finished until more recent times: the builders ran out of funds, and the twin spires – part of the original design – were only completed in the 1990s, when they were lowered on to the building by helicopter.

The highlight of the magnificent interior is the gorgeous terrazzo floor of the crypt, inlaid with Celtic patterns and an illustration of the six days of creation. To gain entry, you will need to buy a ticket from the cathedral shop, near the College Street entrance.

HYDE PARK BARRACKS

From the cathedral, follow Prince Albert Road north to the traffic lights and turn north into Macquarie Street, the closest thing Sydney has to a grand boulevard. In the colony's early days, this was the administrative quarter; today, Sydney's top medical specialists can be found here, their offices housed in a series of beautiful Art Deco edifices.

The building on the corner with College Street is **Hyde Park Barracks ❷** (Queens Square, Macquarie Street; tel: 02 8239 2311; www.hht.net.au; daily 9.30am–5pm; charge). This was the first jail in Australia, opened in 1819, 30 years after the colony's founding. As

Above from far left: St Mary's Cathedral; the CBD by night from above; historic architecture in central Sydney.

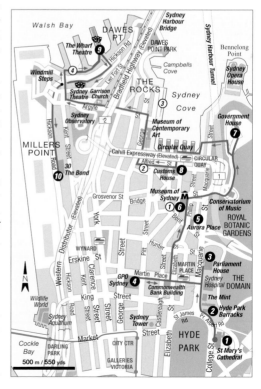

a penal settlement, Sydney had a population that consisted mainly of convicts; however, jails were not seen as a huge priority, as the harsh environment and climate offered would-be escapees nowhere to run to. Ironically, Hyde Park Barracks was designed by a former convict, Francis Greenway *(see margin, left)*, who had been commissioned by Governor Macquarie.

Hyde Park Barracks served as a jail for 30 years, and thereafter as a female immigration depot, an asylum for the aged and infirm, a court and as government buildings. These days, the building houses a changing series of exhibitions dedicated to convict life and the history of the building.

RUM HOSPITAL

Greenway also designed the next three sights: the Mint, Sydney Hospital and Parliament House, which once formed a huge edifice housing Sydney's first hospital. Known as the Rum Hospital, its story reveals a lot about the way the colony was run in its early days.

Three merchants agreed to fund the hospital in return for a monopoly on the importation of rum, the most precious currency of the time. The original building was so shoddily constructed that the main body (now Sydney Hospital) had to be rebuilt under Greenway's direction. The hospital's two wings were eventually requisitioned to serve as the Mint and

Parliament House. Both wings have undergone considerable renovation, but still retain features dating back to 1811 from the original building.

Parliament House

There is something very laidback about New South Wales' **Parliament House** ❸ (Macquarie Street; tel: 02 9230 2111; www.parliament.nsw.gov.au; Mon–Fri 9am–5pm; free). With its double verandas, pastel-coloured awnings and decorative iron-work, it looks like it has been modelled on a typical Queenslander house. The interior feels slightly more formal, taking as its inspiration the interiors of London's Houses of Parliament, right down to the colour scheme (red for the upper chamber, green for the lower).

Tours are available at different times depending on whether Parliament is sitting – see the website for more details. It is also possible to watch proceedings from the public galleries when Parliament is sitting.

MARTIN PLACE

Situated directly opposite Sydney Hospital lies Martin Place, the largest open space in the CBD. The southern side in particular is lined with fine Victorian sandstone buildings erected with the profits of booming wheat and wool industries. One of the most striking is the Commonwealth Bank building between Castlereagh and Elizabeth

Francis Greenway

Francis Greenway was sentenced to 14 years' transportation for forgery in 1814. His design talents were soon recognised by Governor Macquarie, who enlisted Greenway in his building campaign to transform the face of Sydney. Greenway's architectural legacy was so strong that for many years, his portrait appeared on Australia's $10 note: probably the only time the image of a convicted forger has appeared on a country's currency.

streets, one of several buildings that the bank owns along the plaza. Finished in 1928, the neoclassical building has a magnificent interior, including a two-storey marble banking chamber that is visible through the building's windows.

GPO Sydney

You will need to walk all the way down to George Street to see Martin Place's most magnificent monument, but it is well worth the detour. The former General Post Office, known these days as **GPO Sydney** ❹ (1 Martin Place; tel: 02 9229 7700; www.gposydney. com; daily, hours differ according to venue; free) was designed by James Barnet, who was responsible for many of 19th-century Sydney's most elegant buildings. These days, the GPO houses several acclaimed restaurants and bars, including Prime Restaurant and GPO Oyster Bar. Even if you are not hungry, take a walk inside to admire the magnificently restored interior, complete with ornately decorated staircases.

AURORA PLACE

Walk back up Martin Place and turn left when you reach Elizabeth Street. After about 300m/yds you will come to the intersection with Hunter Street. On your right rises one of Sydney's newest landmarks, **Aurora Place** ❺. Walk one block north to reach it, at the junction of Philip Street and Bent

Above from far left: at the Sydney mint; exterior of Hyde Park Barracks; inside the barracks.

Below: office buildings in the CBD.

Street. Designed by acclaimed Italian architect Renzo Piano, it consists of two buildings: a slender 18-storey apartment block and a 41-storey office tower. The glass curtain-wall seems to float independently, while the curves pay homage to the Opera House.

MUSEUM OF SYDNEY

At the next intersection north (ie the one with Bridge Street) is the **Museum of Sydney ❻** (corner of Bridge and Phillip streets; tel: 02 9251 5988; www.hht.net.au; daily 9.30am–5pm; charge), located on the site of the colony's first Government House. Walk through the 29 pillars (representing the 29 local clans) of the *Edge of the Trees* sculpture at the main entrance to hear the names of places from around the metropolis in the Eora languages that were spoken by the area's original Aboriginal inhabitants.

The Museum of Sydney has a variety of changing exhibitions, as well as permanent displays commemorating the 'Sydney Visionaries' who shaped the city, and a gallery dedicated to the local Cadigal people. The stories of individuals such as Patyegarang, Barangaro and Colebee – a tribal chief who was at first imprisoned, but escaped, and later used to dine with Captain Phillip of the First Fleet – are a reminder of how fluid and complex relationships between black and white were in the early days of the colony. The museum's sleek **MOS Cafe**, see ⓜ①, is a popular spot for breakfast and lunch.

CONSERVATORIUM OF MUSIC

From the museum, head up Bridge Street to Macquarie Street. On the opposite side of the road you will see the **Conservatorium of Music** (www.music.usyd.edu.au). The original building, on the left, with crenellated towers, was designed by Francis Greenway to serve as the stables for Government House. Together with the adjoining modern extension, it now houses the city's most talented musical students. Students and staff often perform concerts in the new building and admission fees are modest.

GOVERNMENT HOUSE

Follow the Conservatorium's driveway left into the Royal Botanic Gardens and follow the sign to **Government House ❼** (Macquarie Street; tel: 02 9931 5222; www.hht.net.au; grounds daily 10am–4pm, house open for tours only, Fri–Sun 10.30am–3pm every half-hour; free). Designed by the English architect Edward Blore, who was also involved in the creation of Buckingham Palace in London, this frivolous Romantic mock castle built between 1837 and 1845 is as absurdly out of place as it is charming.

Above: some of the city's historic buildings.

Royal Operation
The drawing room of Government House functioned as a makeshift operating theatre in 1868, following the attempted assassination of Prince Alfred, Queen Victoria's second son. Surgeons commandeered the room when they had to dislodge a bullet from the royal abdomen.

Government House remained the residence of the State Governor until the mid-1990s, when the Labor premier snatched this perk of office away from the incumbent and opened it to the people instead, introducing a programme of cultural events including concerts. The house contains impressive collections of colonial furniture and paintings, as well as contemporary works by NSW artists, craftspeople and designers. A stroll through the historic gardens is recommended.

CUSTOMS HOUSE

Exiting the gates of Government House, take the service road that curves away to the right. This will bring you to another set of gates on to Macquarie Street. Directly across the road is a set of stairs leading down to the harbour. Take the stairs and turn left at the bottom, following the water around to Circular Quay. Walk along Circular Quay until you reach Wharf 4, opposite which stands another of James Barnet's gems, **Customs House** ❽ (31 Alfred Street; tel: 02 9242 8551; www.cityofsydney.nsw.gov.au; Mon–Fri 8am–midnight, Sat 10am–midnight, Sun 11am–5pm; free).

Dating from 1885, this building is reputed to stand on the site where the Union flag was first flown in Sydney. The building's award-winning interiors now contain a full-scale model of the CBD under the floor of the

atrium, some of the city's library collections. There are also various bars and restaurants here *(see margin, right)*.

WALSH BAY

Exiting Customs House, turn left and walk up Alfred Street towards George Street. If you are in need of refreshment, you can stop in at **Tony Bilson's Number One Wine Bar**, see ⑪②, or **Cruise Restaurant**, see ⑪③; alternatively, turn right into George Street

Above from far left:
Government House;
Museum of Sydney.

A Nice Custom
Cafe Sydney (tel: 02 9251 8683; www.cafesydney.com; Mon–Fri L, D; Sat D; Sun L, AT; $$$–$$$$) on the fifth floor of Customs House is great for a drink or an (expensive) meal, with live jazz on Sundays.

Food and Drink

① MOS CAFE
Corner of Bridge and Phillip streets; tel: 02 9241 3636; Mon–Fri B, L, D, Sat–Sun B, L; $$
Sitting in the courtyard enjoying a late breakfast of wood mushroom omelette or creamed eggs with smoked salmon and chives on toast is an eminently civilised way to start the day. The sleek Modern Australian bistro food includes plenty of classy vegetarian options.

② TONY BILSON'S NUMBER ONE WINE BAR
1 Alfred Street; tel: 02 8252 9296; www.numberone winebar.com; Mon–Fri L, D, Sat D; $$–$$$
Tony Bilson is one of Sydney's pioneering chefs, and his new wine bar and restaurant mixes his favoured French influences with sensational Spanish flavours. There are wines from Australia and around the world to suit every price range, from a cheap-as-chips house wine to classic Châteauneuf-du-Pape.

③ CRUISE RESTAURANT
Level 2, Overseas Passenger Terminal; tel: 02 9251 1188; www.cruisebar.com.au; Wed–Fri L, Tue–Sat D; $$–$$$$
With prime views of the Opera House and the harbour, it is no surprise that the chic restaurants in the Overseas Passenger Terminal will never make a cheap-eats list. Cruise remains a favourite, its sophisticated food a match for the splendid view.

Celebrity Boost

The appointment of the actor Cate Blanchett and her playwright husband, Andrew Upton, as co-artistic directors of the Sydney Theatre Company has lifted its international profile, attracting patrons such as Giorgio Armani and performers such as Liv Ullman.

then left at the next intersection. Walk up Argyle Street through the convict-chiselled tunnel called the Argyle Cut, past Observatory Hill on your left and the Garrison Church on your right. Turn right into Kent Street and after a block you will come to Windmill Steps, which take you down into Walsh Bay (www.walshbaysydney.com.au).

From here, turn right and walk along the wharves. The third wharf you come to is **The Wharf Theatre ❾** (Pier 4–5 Hickson Road; tel: 02 9250 1777; www.sydneytheatre.com.au; daily; free), the original home of the **Sydney Theatre Company** (STC; *see margin, left*). Even if you are not catching a performance, it is worth going upstairs and walking all the way along the atmospheric corridor lined with massive timber beams down to where The Wharf restaurant enjoys a magnificent water view.

On the other side of the road, slightly to the south, is the STC's newer venue, **Sydney Theatre**, which is also worth a peek. The theatre occupies a former Bond Stores (warehouse), and the

design has kept old distressed walls, as well as recycling original timbers to stunning effect.

The wharves opposite the Sydney Theatre have been redeveloped to cater for Sydney's insatiable hunger for luxury waterfront living. The complexes host several pleasant wine bars and restaurants, most notably **Ventuno**, see Ⓨ④.

30 The Bond

You can either finish the walk here or, if you have the energy, head south along Hickson Road, veering left at the lights, for about 600m/yds. On the left is **30 The Bond ❿**, the headquarters of property group LendLease: the first office building in central Sydney to achieve a five-star energy rating, and one of the city's most impressive modern buildings. The external stairs alongside seem to float in the air, while the back wall of the atrium is a four-storey convict-hewn sandstone wall (take a peek through the building's glass walls near the stairs).

From here, you can easily return to the city centre by taking the stairs or the lift to the top of the plateau. Head right and then left into Gas Lane, which will bring you up to Kent Street. Cross the road and follow the path heading south to reach Clarence Street. At the second set of lights, turn left into Margaret Street and walk two blocks up to George Street. Three blocks further west is Wynyard station.

Food and Drink

④ VENTUNO

21 Hickson Road; tel: 02 9247 4444; www.ventuno. com.au; daily L, D; $$

This stylish yet relaxed eatery specialises in pizza, but also offers a broad array of pasta and meat dishes. Its indoor-outdoor setting makes it the perfect place to while away a balmy night or a lazy Sunday afternoon.

DARLING HARBOUR

For years a derelict harbourside neighbourhood, Darling Harbour is now one of the city's most visited areas. From family-friendly attractions to bars, museums and even a casino, it has more than enough to fill a day.

4

Hidden behind the city's skyscrapers, the Darling Harbour precinct has reinvented itself a number of times over the last 20 years. The first stage, Darling Harbour itself, was redeveloped as a family destination in time for the bicentennial in 1988. Since then, it has been joined by two cityside precincts, Cockle Bay and King Street wharves, which feature a number of popular restaurants and bars. This tour takes in the highlights of all three, as well as the surrounding area.

SYDNEY AQUARIUM

Australia is an island continent, and the **Sydney Aquarium** ❶ (Aquarium Pier, Darling Harbour; tel: 133 FUN; www.sydneyaquarium.com.au; daily 9am–8pm; charge) showcases the astonishing creatures that inhabit the waters around the continent and also around the world.

Begin by inspecting the 50 tanks that hold around 5,000 sea creatures, from blue starfish the size of a dinner plate to saltwater crocodiles. The main attractions, however, are the two floating oceaniums. One is home to rare dugongs, a marine mammal found

> **DISTANCE** 4.25km (2⅔ miles)
> **TIME** A full day
> **START** Sydney Aquarium
> **END** Pyrmont Bridge
> **POINTS TO NOTE**
> You can reach the Aquarium either by walking west down Market Street, or catching the monorail to Darling Park. If you do this walk in the week, attractions such as the Aquarium and the Chinese Garden will be less crowded; at weekends, the crowds are larger, but there will be street entertainment to enjoy.

in the waters of North Australia; the other contains a vast number of sharks and giant rays, which are viewed from transparent underwater tunnels. There can be long queues for the oceanariums, but they are worth it: the sight of these enormous creatures floating by just metres away is not one you will forget in a hurry.

WILDLIFE WORLD

Once you surface from your underwater explorations, it is on to the terrestrial

Above from far left: the Sydney Theatre Company; admiring the sharks through transparent underwater tunnels at the aquarium.

Monorail
This relatively compact area is easy to negotiate on foot, but a monorail loops around Darling Harbour (travelling anticlockwise only), and the tram (LightRail) service that runs from Central Railway along the western edge of Darling Harbour is useful for getting to the Powerhouse and Sydney Fish Market. For more information on either service, visit www.metrotransport. com.au.

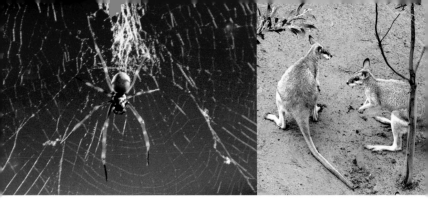

delights of **Wildlife World** ❷ (Aquarium Pier, Darling Harbour; tel: 133 FUN; www.sydneywildlifeworld.com.au; daily 9am–5pm; charge), right next door. Australia's many weird and wonderful species of wildlife are on display, from its venomous spiders to its astonishing array of reptiles; the continent has 840 reptile species, compared with just 280 in North America. Australia also has the most poisonous species of snakes in the world.

There is also a collection of nocturnal animals, Australia being the only continent to have more animals active by night than by day. As well as special koala and kangaroo enclosures, there are nine unique Australian habitats, from wallaby-filled grasslands to the tropical rainforest where you can walk surrounded by thousands of colourful butterflies. From ghost bats and bilbies to wombats and cassowaries, this place has them all.

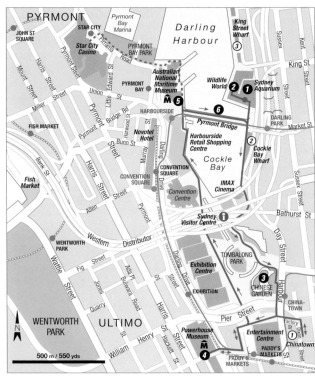

CHINESE GARDEN

From here, follow the water's edge south, heading inland past the IMAX 3-D cinema and the old-fashioned carousel, to the children's play area. Veer left and follow the signs for the **Chinese Garden ③** (tel: 02 9240 8888; daily 9.30am–5pm; charge).

A bicentennial gift from the government of China's Guangdong province, the garden is an enchanting confection of ponds clad with water lilies and picturesque wooden bridges, and plants including four types of bamboo, evergreen pines and willows, the flowering apricot (the national flower of China) and red silk cotton trees (the floral emblem of Guangdong). End your visit with tea in the traditional teahouse.

CHINATOWN

Now continue south, following the signs to the Entertainment Centre. Cross Harbour Street and walk up Factory Street to reach Dixon Street, the heart of Sydney's Chinatown. If you are hungry, there are countless eateries to choose from here, including **Superbowl**, see ⓘ① . The food court on the corner of Dixon and Factory streets also offers cheap-and-cheerful meals.

POWERHOUSE MUSEUM

Now head back to the Entertainment Centre and, skirting its northern side,

walk past the car park until you come to the steps leading up to the footbridge next to Paddy's Market monorail. Walk across to the western side, turn left and you'll reach the sprawling **Powerhouse Museum ④** (500 Harris Street Ultimo; tel: 02 9217 0111; daily 10am–5pm, www.phm.gov. au; charge), one of Australia's best.

Its brief covers science, technology, decorative arts and popular culture; over the years, it has featured exhibits on topics from Kylie Minogue's stage costumes to artificial intelligence and the history of housework. The interactive approach makes it fun for families. The permanent exhibitions alone could easily take half a day to explore.

Space and Transport

The museum's Space exhibition features everything from rocket motors to shuttle tiles, spacesuits and a moon rock. The highlight is a **Zero Gravity Space Lab** that creates the illusion of being in a weightless environment. The Transport gallery on Level 1 covers more conventional vehicles, from hansom

Above from far left: spiders, wallabies and a cassowary at Wildlife World; the Chinese Garden.

Eastern Heritage

The history of the Chinese in Australia goes back almost 200 years, with the earliest record of a Chinese settler dating back to 1818. The 1850s Gold Rush drew thousands more, while the 1990s and early 21st century have seen another influx. According to the last census, 7 percent of Sydneysiders have a Chinese heritage.

Food and Drink

① SUPERBOWL
41 Dixon Street, Chinatown; tel: 02 9281 2462; daily L, D; $–$$
A great example of the no-frills dining that Chinatown does so well. There is plenty of Cantonese seafood and barbecue on offer, as well as provincial specials such as shredded jellyfish. The house speciality is *congee*, a savoury rice porridge.

Above from left:
evidence of Australia's
naval history at the
Maritime Museum;
Darling Harbour at
night.

cabs and vintage motorcycles to various kinds of aeroplane. The first train ever used in Australia, Locomotive Number One, is displayed on Level 3.

Sustainability and Innovation

Ecologic, an exhibit devoted to sustainability, highlights the changes we can make to our lifestyles and industries to protect the environment. Its fascinating exhibits include details on how to make each room of our house more environmentally friendly, to a breakdown of what is really involved in the production, packaging and transport in a single packet of Kettle Chips. The **Success and Innovations** exhibit looks at some of Australia's most successful industrial designs, from Victa lawnmowers to the world's first animated superstar, Felix the Cat. Kids will love the hands-on exhibits, including one that lets them try their hand at shearing an electronic sheep.

Experimentations, Chemical Attractions and Steam Engines

Another favourite with children is the **Experimentations** section, which has more than 30 interactive exhibits that demonstrate the principles of temperature and pressure, electricity and magnetism, light, gravity and motion, and chemistry.

The **Chemical Attractions** section, which looks at how chemicals are used in everyday products to stimulate our senses, is also popular – predictably, the chocolate exhibit is particularly so.

The museum's most valuable exhibit – part of its display dedicated to the steam revolution – is the Boulton and Watt steam engine, the oldest surviving rotational steam engine in the world. The museum also has play areas for younger children, and a courtyard cafe that's a great place to take a break.

Below: displays
at the Power-
house Museum.

VH-UAU

AUSTRALIAN NATIONAL MARITIME MUSEUM

Leaving the museum, retrace your route along the footbridge. At the bottom of the stairs, head north back towards Darling Harbour itself and the Harbourside Festival Market Place. At its northern end lies the **Australian National Maritime Museum** ❺ (2 Murray Street, Darling Harbour; tel: 02 9298 3777; www.anmm.gov.au; daily 9.30am–5pm; charge). Inside, exhibits are grouped thematically in categories such as discovery, commerce, defence and leisure. The most moving exhibition, about human migration, traces the voyages of convicts, free settlers, post-World War II European immigrants and refugees from the Vietnam War.

A range of working vessels is exhibited both inside and outside the museum, from a Vietnamese fishing boat to the *Australia II* yacht, which won the 1983 America's Cup on a wave of national jubilation.

PYRMONT BRIDGE

If you feel the need to offload some cash, head west from the museum along Pirrama Road to the **Star City Casino** (80 Pyrmont Street, Pyrmont; tel: 02 9777 9000; www.starcity.com.au; daily 24 hours; free), housing theatres and restaurants as well as gaming tables and slot machines.

Otherwise, head back to Cockle Bay Wharf via **Pyrmont Bridge** ❻. The first bridge built here was a private toll one: pedestrians paid tuppence each way, while sheep and pigs were charged a farthing a head. The current structure was considered a masterpiece of modern engineering when it opened in 1902, with an 800-tonne, 70m (230ft) electronic 'swing span' that pivots horizontally to let large vessels enter the inner harbour.

Finish off the walk either with a meal at **Chinta Ria**, see 🍴②, or head north along the water to King Street Wharf, where you can relax in one of the area's many bars and restaurants, such as **The Loft**, see 🍴③.

Fantastic Fish
Gourmets should hop on the LightRail and head for the Sydney Fish Market (corner of Pyrmont Bridge Road and Bank Street, Blackwattle Bay; tel: 02 9004 1100; daily 7am–4pm). This is the largest seafood market outside Japan and trades around 15 million kg (33 million lbs) of seafood a year. Sydneysiders flock here to scoop up ocean-fresh oysters, prawns and fish, or just to enjoy some fresh-cooked seafood.

Food and Drink 🍴

② CHINTA RIA... TEMPLE OF LOVE
Roof Terrace, Cockle Bay Wharf; tel: 02 9264 3211; www.chintaria.com.au; daily L, D; $$
The jolly giant Buddha beaming benevolently over the room sets the tone for this buzzing restaurant specialising in Malaysian hawker-style food. Favourites such as satays and roti are perfectly done, and other dishes are fragrant with flavours of tamarind, coriander and coconut.

③ THE LOFT
3 Lime Street, King Street Wharf; tel: 02 9299 4770; www.theloftsydney.com.au; Mon–Thur D, Fri–Sun L, D; $$
Luscious leather sofas, floral fretwork on the ceilings and walls and geometric cut-out screens in rich burnt colours give The Loft a 21st-century Moroccan feel. The sophisticated young crowd indulging in tapas such as the Asian platter – tempura prawns, sticky Mongolian pork ribs, sushi – or the South American platter – spicy empanadas, chilli- and chocolate-glazed pork strips – and cocktails has included international guests such as Prince Harry.

ELIZABETH BAY
TO SURRY HILLS

A walk through Sydney's trendy inner-city suburbs is a study in contrasts. From graceful 19th-century architecture to hip bars and cafes, pocket-sized boutiques to world-class dining, it offers a slice of real Sydney life.

DISTANCE 5km (3 miles)
TIME A half-day
START Elizabeth Bay House
END Crown Street
POINTS TO NOTE

To reach Elizabeth Bay House, take bus no. 311 from the city (see www.131500.info), and ask to be let out at the closest stop. This tour has two endings, depending on how far you feel like walking. In either case, start the tour in the afternoon, and you will be able to finish with a drink in one of the city's hip bars, either in Darlinghurst or Surry Hills. If you want to take in the Brett Whiteley studio *(see box, p.58)*, do the tour on a weekend. The shorter version of this walk can be combined with tour 6 (Paddington and Woollahra, *see p.60*).

Neighbourhood Watch

Even in the 1830s, Potts Point – then known as Woolloomooloo Hill – was subject to planning controls. Anyone who received a land grant in the area had conditions imposed on their houses, including the budget (at least £1,000), the orientation (facing the city) and an approvals process (the Governor had to approve the design).

There are few monuments or museums in Sydney's inner suburbs, but a few hours spent wandering the streets of Potts Point, Kings Cross, Darlinghurst and Surry Hills offers one of the best insights into Sydney's vibrant and diverse heart. The sleaze of the Kings Cross strip blends into chic Potts Point at one end and hip Darlinghurst at the other, while the backstreets of 'the Cross' house some of the city's most elegant residential architecture. Some of the main sights along the way are indicated, but the real joy of this walk is soaking up the inner-city vibe, stopping off at whichever cafes, boutiques or galleries catch your eye.

ELIZABETH BAY HOUSE

The grandest house in town when it was built in 1839, **Elizabeth Bay House** ❶ (7 Onslow Avenue, Elizabeth Bay; tel: 02 9356 3022; www.hht.net.au; Fri–Sun 9.30am–4pm; charge) gives a sense of how the colony's elite used to live. The design is attributed to John Verge, but the original owner, Colonial Secretary Alexander Macleay, drove down every day during the four-year construction period to supervise the work personally. The house's most magnificent feature is an elliptical saloon dominated by a curving cantilevered staircase under

a dome. Macleay was only able to enjoy the house for a few years before his son, from whom he'd borrowed much of the money to finance the house, took occupancy, sending his father to live with his sister.

Elizabeth Bay House was once famous for its 22 hectares (54 acres) of gardens, which included orchards, flower gardens, a kitchen garden and a vast collection of native and exotic plants. Most of the gardens are now covered by apartment blocks; the pocket park opposite the house itself, with its pretty grotto, is one of the few visible remnants.

TOWARDS POTTS POINT

On leaving Elizabeth Bay House, turn right into Onslow Avenue and follow the road around 100m/yds up to the intersection with Elizabeth Bay Road and Greenknowe Avenue. Near the

Above from far left: ibis at Elizabeth Bay House; the colonial-style front of Elizabeth Bay House; sitting by the dandelion-shaped El Alamein Fountain in Potts Point (see p.56).

Below left: Elizabeth Bay House's fabulous cantilevered staircase and dome.

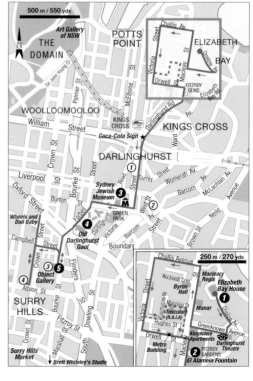

Local Landmark

The Coca-Cola sign at the Cross is the largest billboard in the southern hemisphere, with a total length of 41m/yds and 13m (40ft) in height.

intersection with Onslow Avenue, on the south side of Greenknowe Avenue, is **Darlinghurst Theatre**, one of the city's premier performance venues for independent drama.

Macleay Street

Turn right and head up Greenknowe Avenue to Macleay Street, the heart of the chic enclave of **Potts Point**, known for its lively cafes and restaurants as well as some of the city's most attractive residential architecture. Just before the intersection with Macleay are the ornate **Kingsclere Apartments**, one of the first high-rise apartment blocks of flats in Sydney. Built in 1912, the exclusive apartments each had two balconies and two bathrooms, wood panelling and automatic passenger lifts.

As you head north down Macleay Street, you will see more grand apartment buildings from the 1920s and 1930s, including the **Macleay Regis** at no. 122, **Byron Hall** at no. 97–9, and **Manar** at no. 42.

Victoria Street

Turn left into Challis Avenue then, at the end of the street, left into Victoria Street. The grand Greek Revival houses in Challis Avenue and the imposing terraces on Victoria Street in this inner-city suburb of Potts Point were threatened by developers in the 1960s and 1970s. Like the old houses in The Rocks *(see p.28)*, they were saved from developers by the 'green

bans', imposed by the Builders' Labourers Federation. Their members supported the protests of the local community by refusing to work on the threatened sites. Among the prominent local supporters of the green bans was heiress Juanita Nielsen, who lived at 202 Victoria Street. As proprietor of a local newspaper, she fought against the developers, which is widely assumed to be the reason for her disappearance, and presumed murder, in July 1975.

Hughes, Orwell, Tusculum
and Manning Streets

Walk along the plane-tree-lined Victoria Street for about 200m/yds, before turning left up either Hughes or Orwell Street. Orwell Street is home to Art Deco buildings including the curving **Metro Building** on your left, where Australia's premiere of the musical *Hair* provoked outrage in the 1960s.

Alternatively, head up Hughes Street and turn left into Tusculum Street, then right into Manning Street, to admire the elegant facade of **Tusculum**, another of the mansions Verge designed for the area. Today Tusculum is home to the Royal Australian Institute of Architects.

KINGS CROSS

Both Hughes and Orwell streets lead back to Macleay Street. Head south past the city's most distinctive fountain, the dandelion-shaped **El Alamein Fountain ❷**, which marks the division

between genteel Potts Point and the more raucous Kings Cross and commemorates the soldiers who died during the two battles at El Alamein in Egypt during World War II.

Follow Darlinghurst Road up to the Cross itself, the intersection of five streets dominated by a massive neon Coca-Cola sign *(see margin, left)*.

A History of Vice

Originally as upmarket as the neighbouring areas, 'the Cross', as it is commonly known, developed a bohemian reputation in the 1930s and 1940s, attracting poets and painters such as Mary Gilmore and William Dobell. Artist Donald Friend reminisced about the 'genuine Berlin air' of the Cross in the 1940s, describing it as a place where 'everybody is wicked'. The area's proximity to the Garden Island naval base and the Woolloomooloo docks made it a popular recreation spot for servicemen during World War II and the Vietnam War, leading to the introduction of the strip clubs that, along with backpacker hostels, now characterise the main drag.

A series of plaques on the footpath commemorates the area's history, including the first gay protest march in 1978 that evolved into the annual Gay Mardi Gras parade.

DARLINGHURST

Continue straight on from the Cross (confusingly, at this point Darlinghurst Road splits into two). Take the left-hand fork – Victoria Street, which from here to Liverpool Street is packed with boutiques and cafes, including **Tropicana Caffe**, see ①①, and, a few blocks down Liverpool Street, **Bill's**, see ①②.

Sydney Jewish Museum

From Victoria Street, turn right into Burton Street and walk up a block. On the corner with Darlinghurst Road is the **Sydney Jewish Museum** ❸ (148

Above: welcome to 'the Cross'.

Food and Drink

① TROPICANA CAFFE
227 Victoria Street, Darlinghurst; tel: 02 9360 9809; www.tropicana caffe.com; daily B, L, D; $
There is nothing flash about this local favourite, but it is still the place to stop for a coffee or a hearty salad. The world's largest short film festival, Tropfest, held every February, is named after the cafe, where it was first held.

② BILL'S
433 Liverpool Street, Darlinghurst; tel: 02 9360 9631; www.bills.com. au; daily B, L; $–$$
Chef Bill Granger owes his fame to his cookbooks and television appearances. His oldest Sydney outlet (there are three) is on this sunny corner terrace. It serves one of Sydney's best brunches; ricotta hotcakes with fresh banana and honeycomb butter, and sweetcorn fritters with roast tomato, spinach and bacon.

Market Day
On the first Saturday of each month, the community comes out to play at Surry Hills Market. The emphasis is on pre-loved and handmade goods, and the location is the Shannon Reserve on the corner of Crown and Collins streets.

Darlinghurst Road; tel: 02 9360 7999; www.sydneyjewishmuseum.com.au; Mon–Thur 10am–4pm, Fri 10am–2pm, Sun 10am–4pm; charge). The main exhibits focus on the Holocaust, but part of the museum is devoted to the history of Jewish life in Australia, from the arrival of the First Fleet – which carried 16 Jewish convicts – to the present day; there is also a kosher cafe.

Darlinghurst Gaol

The magnificent collection of sandstone buildings on the block bounded by Darlinghurst, Burton and Forbes streets is the **Old Darlinghurst Gaol** ❹. Today it is home to the National Art School, and closed to the public, but looking through the gates on Burton Street will give you a sense of the scale of the place.

Begun in 1822, the first cellblocks were completed in 1840 and the first inmates moved in the following year. Construction continued around them until the gaol was completed in 1885. Seventy-nine people were hanged at Darlinghurst Gaol, the last in 1907. Crowds would gather at nearby Green Park to view the hanging, which took place on a platform high enough to be visible above the prison's high walls.

SURRY HILLS

You can either finish your walk here, with a drink in one of the venues on Victoria Street or Darlinghurst Road, or walk south a little further down Forbes Street to reach Oxford Street, one of Sydney's most famous thoroughfares. For years, the lower end of

Brett Whiteley's Studio

There is something so reflective of Sydney about Brett Whiteley's work, from the dazzling blue harbourscapes (such as his *Opera House*, shown right) to the whimsical yet philosophical matchsticks sculpture outside the Art Gallery of NSW *(see p.40)*. One of the most talented Australian artists to emerge in the early 1960s, Whiteley struggled with heroin addiction for 20 years before his death, aged 53, in 1992; some of his inner turmoil was reflected in his work. His studio (2 Raper Street, Surry Hills; tel: 02 9225 1881; www.brettwhiteley.org; Sat–Sun 10am–4pm; free) features changing exhibitions, and curious collections of objects are arranged as displays in themselves. It is accessible from this tour; from Bourke Street *(see opposite)*, turn right into Davies, then Raper Street is the second on your left.

kings Cross has been home to many people

WEALTHY, RESPECTABLE, IMPOVERISHED, BOHEMIAN A **JUST PLAIN CRIMINAL.**

Residents know well the nuances of its streets.

Oxford Street was Sydney's gay golden mile, while the upper end constitutes one of Sydney's most exclusive shopping precincts. The lower end is now a bit tawdry, but the side streets of Surry Hills offer plenty of opportunities for shopping, eating and browsing.

St Margarets Complex

At the lights cross and walk south down Bourke Street about 100m/yds to **St Margarets Complex**, a former hospital that is now home to the **Object Gallery** ➎ (417 Bourke Street, Surry Hills; tel: 02 9361 4511; www.object.com.au; Tue–Fri 11am–5pm, Sat–Sun 10am–5pm; free). The gallery features the best of Australian craft and design, and is housed in a chapel formerly used by nuns. The complex also houses some cafes, including **Pizza Mario**, see ①③.

Crown Street

To continue, head north back along Bourke Street and west at Campbell Street to reach Crown Street, which is home to an ever-changing roster of boutiques, restaurants and cafes. Head north to find boutiques such as **Wheels and Doll Baby** at 259 Crown Street, which has been delivering rock-chick chic for years. The label has now gone global, but this is the store where it all started.

Alternatively, for some of Sydney's best food and drink options, head south along Crown Street to find Sydney foodies' favourites such as **Billy Kwong**, see ①④, with chef Kylie Kwong wowing diners with her modern Chinese food. When you are ready, return to Oxford Street to catch a bus heading back to town.

Above from far left:
Darlinghurst Gaol;
Crown Street is
known for its chic
fashion boutiques;
commemorative
plaque in Kings Cross
(see p.57).

Food and Drink

③ PIZZA MARIO
St Margarets, 417–21 Bourke Street, Surry Hills; tel: 02 9332 3633;
www.pizzamario.com.au; daily D; $$
As the name suggests, pizza is the main game here, with the dining room run by two card-carrying members of the Associazione Verace Pizza Napoletana (AVPN), a society dedicated to delivering authentic Neapolitan pizza. The other dishes, including perfectly fried calamari, are just as authentic.

④ BILLY KWONG
335 Crown Street, Surry Hills; tel: 02 9332 3300; www.kyliekwong.org/
BillyKwongs/aspx; daily D; $$–$$$
To get into Kylie Kwong's tiny dining room, you will either need to show up early or be prepared to wait; the restaurant doesn't take bookings, and by the 6pm opening time a queue will already have formed. The food, however, such as the excellent crispy-skin duck with fresh blood-orange sauce and lamb with plum sauce, is well worth the inconvenience.

PADDINGTON AND WOOLLAHRA

These two upmarket neighbourhoods are ground zero for Sydney's fashion and art scenes. Check out global names such as Collette Dinnigan and Akira Isogawa, as well as the next big thing at Paddington Markets.

Paddington Pubs

Tucked away in the backstreets of Paddington is an impressive collection of British-style pubs, all with quality restaurants as well as cosy bars. From the Boddington's ale to the pommy accents, it is enough to make you feel you are in Blighty. If you are in the mood for a pint with a side order of nostalgia, choose between the Four in Hand (105 Sutherland Street; tel: 02 9362 1999; www.fourin hand.com.au), the Royal Hotel (237 Glenmore Road; tel: 02 9331 2604; www.royalhotel. com.au), the Grand National (161 Underwood Street; tel: 02 9363 4557) and the Lord Dudley (236 Jersey Road; tel: 02 9327 5399; www. lorddudley.com.au).

DISTANCE 8km (5 miles)

TIME A full day

START Victoria Barracks

END Woollahra

POINTS TO NOTE

From the city, catch a bus going to Oxford Street and ask to be let off at the Victoria Barracks stop. The tour is best done on a Saturday in order to visit Paddington Markets; allow a couple of hours to see the markets in full, if possible.

Once a notorious slum, Paddington is now one of Sydney's most glittering neighbourhoods. Oxford Street is Sydney's golden mile for shopping, while the suburb's backstreets are lined with terraces, trees and charming boutiques and galleries. Yet like much of Sydney, Paddington's early history is dominated by the military.

VICTORIA BARRACKS

This walk starts at **Victoria Barracks** ❶ (corner of Oxford Street and Greens Road; tel: 02 8335 5170; Thur tour 10am; museum 10am–3pm; free), built to replace the existing barracks near Wynyard station. The site was chosen because it was accessible to both the harbour and Botany Bay. Work began in 1841 and was due to be completed in two and a half years; ultimately, it took three times as long. The Barracks opened in 1848 and are still a working site, as well as housing a museum that will appeal to those with a bent for uniforms, guns and medals. The guards on duty wear traditional colonial uniforms. Many of the cottages built to house the convict workforce can still be seen in the streets that run off Oxford Street opposite the barracks, such as Bourke Lane and Shadforth Street.

GLENMORE ROAD

Heading east on Oxford Street, the second street on your left after Greens Road is **Glenmore Road** ❷. This was Paddington's first major road, created by the bullock carts hauling gin to Oxford Street from the Glenmore Distillery near Rushcutters Bay.

Today the stretch of Glenmore Road adjoining Oxford Street is home to some of Sydney's most stylish clothing shops, along with some quality art galleries.

Chic Boutiques

Fashionistas will want to check out designers such as **Kirrily Johnston** at no. 6 (tel: 02 9380 7775; www.kirrily johnston.com; Mon–Sat 10am–6pm, Sun 11am–5pm), known for luxurious, flowing fabrics and feminine designs; **Ginger and Smart** at no. 16a (tel: 02 9380 9966; www.gingerandsmart.com; Mon–Sat 10am–6pm, Sun 11am–5pm), known for their eclectic fabrics and creative colours; and celebrity favourites **Camilla and Marc** (8/2–16 Glenmore Road; tel: 02 9331 1133; www.camillaandmarc.com; Mon–Wed and Fri, Sat 10am–6pm, Thur 10am–7pm, Sun 11am–5pm), whose designs are worn by paparazzi darlings Elle Macpherson, Jennifer Lopez and Lindsay Lohan.

Art Galleries

Also on this stretch are a couple of excellent galleries. At no. 20, **Gallery Savah** (tel: 02 360 9979; www.savah.com.au; Tue–Sun 11am–6pm) represents a selection of notable Australian and Aboriginal artists, while on the opposite side of the street at no. 19, Maunsell Wickes at **Barry Stern Gallery** (tel: 02 9331 4676; www.maunsellwickes.com; Tue–Sat 11am–5.30pm, Sun noon–5pm) sprawls through three 1840s ter-

Above from far left: the area attracts a young fashionable crowd; Paddington boutique; strolling through Paddington.

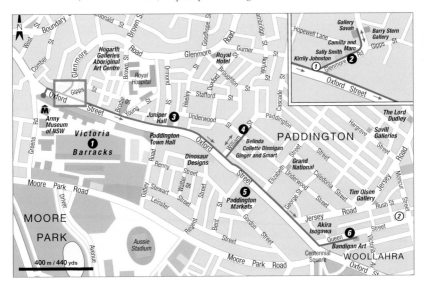

Paddington Galleries

A number of Paddington's best galleries are located away from the main drag. Art-lovers are advised to check out Savill Galleries (156 Hargrave Street; tel: 02 9327 8311; www.savill.com.au) and Tim Olsen Gallery (63 Jersey Road; tel: 02 9327 3922; www. timolsengallery.com) for 20th-century Australian art. Also worth visiting is Hogarth Galleries Aboriginal Art Centre (7 Walker Lane; tel: 02 9360 6839; www. aboriginalartcentres. com), Australia's oldest Aboriginal fine-art gallery.

race houses, with nine exhibition spaces featuring a range of painters, print-makers, sculptors and ceramicists.

If all the art is making you work up a thirst, take a break at **Jackies and Raw Bar II**, see ⑪①, on the corner.

JUNIPER HALL

Head southeast on Oxford Street for about 300m/yds passing the 1891 Italianate **Paddington Town Hall** on the opposite side of the street, to come to the intersection with Ormond Street. This is the location of Paddington's finest historic building, **Juniper Hall** ❸, constructed by Robert Cooper, ex-convict and gin distiller, who received the first land grant in the area.

His elegant villa – named after the key ingredient in gin – was completed in 1824. It housed Cooper's family –

which included his third wife, their 14 children plus another 10 children from his two previous marriages – until their children's extravagance forced the Coopers to rent out the property. Juniper Hall is Australia's oldest surviving villa, although the magnificent views it once enjoyed of Sydney Harbour, Botany Bay and the Blue Mountains have been eaten up by urban sprawl. The building belongs to the National Trust (www.nsw.national trust.org.au) and is currently tenanted by a French antiques store.

Directly opposite, on the corner of Oxford and Oatley Streets, is the former **Paddington Reservoir**, now reinvented as a tranquil sunken garden fringed with a hanging garden canopy. It's a lovely example of urban reinvention, and a favourite spot for locals.

WILLIAM STREET

Around 300m/yds further along and on the left is **William Street** ❹, a terraced strip that is home to many of Paddington's biggest names in fashion. Look for **Collette Dinnigan** at no. 33 (tel: 02 9360 6691; www.collette dinnigan.com.au; Mon–Wed and Fri–Sat 10am–6pm, Thur 10am–7pm, Sun 11am–5pm), who has won global acclaim for her exquisite evening wear; and at no.39, **Belinda** (tel: 02 9380 8728; www.belinda.com.au; Mon–Wed and Fri 10am–6pm, Thur 10am–9pm, Sat 10am–5pm, Sun noon–5pm),

whose boutiques (there are also two in Double Bay) are known for their well-edited choice of up-and-coming and established European labels.

PADDINGTON MARKETS

Back on Oxford Street and slightly further south are **Paddington Markets** ❺ (395 Oxford Street; tel: 02 9331 2923; www.paddingtonmarkets.com.au; Sat 10am–5pm), held in the grounds of the Uniting Church since 1973. Sydney's most famous market has been the launching point for many great Australian labels, including Zimmermann, Dinosaur Designs and Lonely Planet, and some of those names now on William Street (see opposite).

There are around 250 stalls here, selling everything from pet accessories to homemade jams, but the emphasis is on fashions by young designers. The market also has a range of food and drink stalls, and a children's play area. The crowds will slow you right down, so be prepared for this.

WOOLLAHRA

Return to Oxford Street and browse the shops as you head southeast to **Queen Street** ❻, another of the area's great shopping strips, about 500m/yds away. The area you are now in is Woollahra, where the feel is different; the shady trees and larger terraces signal serious money, as does the shopping.

Queen Street is lined with boutiques and galleries, including **Akira Isogawa** (12a Queen Street; tel: 02 9361 5221; www.akira.au.com; Mon–Sat 10.30am–6pm, Sun 11am–4pm), whose ethereal draped outfits have made him one of Australia's most acclaimed designers. Artworks of a different type can be found at the **Dickerson Gallery** (34 Queen Street, Woollahra; tel: 02 9363 3358; www.dickersongallery.com.au; Tue–Sat 11am–5pm, Sun 1–5.30pm), which showcases established and up and coming Australian artists.

At the end of the tour, you might like to grab a bite to eat and a refreshing beverage at the Woollahra Hotel, home to **Bistro Moncur**, see ⑪②.

Above from far left: chi-chi boutique; Paddington Markets.

Opposite below: Juniper Hall.

Dinosaur Designs

Close to Paddington Markets is Australia's best-known jeweller, Dinosaur Designs (339 Oxford Street; tel: 02 9361 3776; www. dinosaurdesigns.com. au; Mon–Wed and Fri 9.30am–5.30pm, Thur 9.30am–8pm, Sat 10am–5pm, Sun noon–4pm), known for their brilliantly coloured, moulded resin jewellery and homewares.

Food and Drink ⑪

① JACKIES AND RAW BAR II
122 Oxford Street, Paddington; tel: 02 9380 9818; Sun–Mon B, L, Wed–Sat B, L, D; $–$$
Once a much-loved Bondi favourite, Jackie's has retained its popularity since relocating to a chic new home, where fashionistas rest their Jimmy Choo shoes either in the large courtyard or the cool sandstone-lined interior. Foodwise, choose from the Italian-influenced cafe menu, or the super-fresh sushi and sashimi.

② BISTRO MONCUR
Woollahra Hotel, 116 Queen Street; tel: 02 9327 9713; www.woollahrahotel.com.au; Tue–Sun L, D, Mon D; $$–$$$
Although actually a pub, Bistro Moncur has a jazzy Parisian feel that is matched by the superb food on offer – far superior to your average pub grub. If you are not in the mood for a full sit-down affair, its more casual option, The Terrace, serves Wagyu burgers and spatchcock.

HERMITAGE FORESHORE

The easy Hermitage foreshore walk, from Rose Bay to Nielsen Park, is one of the prettiest stretches of Sydney's bush-fringed harbour foreshore. Bring a swimsuit to take advantage of the little beaches along the way.

DISTANCE 3km (1¾ miles)
TIME A half-/full day
START Foreshore Reserve
END Vaucluse House
POINTS TO NOTE
Take bus no. 324 from town (see www.131500.com.au for more information) and ask to be let off at Kincoppal. At the end of the walk, you can either take the 324 back to town from outside Vaucluse House, or go on to tour 8 *(see p.66)* by hopping onto the 324 on the opposite side of the road for the short trip to Watsons Bay. Pack sunscreen, water and a hat.

Alight from the no. 324 bus when you see an impressive edifice, reminiscent of a fortified French château, on the corner of New South Head Road and Bayview Hill Road. Originally built as a convent by the Order of the Sacred Heart, it now houses one of Sydney's most exclusive private girls' schools, Kincoppal, where high fees buy you, among other things, stellar harbour views.

Head down Bayview Hill Road, following the road to the right. Where it culminates in a cul de sac, you will find the entrance to the **Foreshore Reserve** ❶. A signposted walk was established through the reserve in 1984; until then, most of the foreshore land had been occupied by property owners.

FORESHORE WALK

This 2km (1¼-mile) dirt track takes you through leafy bush and right along the harbour foreshore. In addition to offering stunning views stretching back to the Harbour Bridge and the Opera House, the walk is the only way to access some of Sydney's least-known beaches; tiny strips of bush-fringed white sand including Queens Beach, Hermit Point Beach and Milk Beach. These make great rest stops along the way, and, on weekdays especially, you will probably have them all to yourself.

Strickland House

Towards the end of the walk, the trail borders the green lawns of **Strickland House** ❷, which had a cameo role in Baz Luhrmann's film *Australia*. The Italianate mansion was designed in 1856 by John Hilly for John Hosking, the first Lord Mayor of Sydney. Its

name was changed from Carrara to Strickland House in 1915, when it became a public convalescent home. These days it is hired out for events, and is not open to the public.

Shark Beach

The foreshore walk culminates at the picturesque **Shark Beach** ❸ (popularly known as Nielsen Park Beach). Do not let the name – and the shark net – worry you: the harbour waters are very safe (the last shark attack in Sydney Harbour was in 1963). **The Beach House**, see ⑪①, is a good pitstop here.

Shell middens and hand stencils testify to the presence of the Cadigal clan in the days before settlement. The beach was once privately owned, but in the early 1900s, boating picnickers were ordered off the beach and drowned while trying to find alternative shelter; the incident added to the demand to make foreshore lands available to all.

Nielsen Park itself was created in 1912 and its shady lawns and kiosk still make it a popular destination.

VAUCLUSE HOUSE

From the top of Nielsen Park, it is just a few minutes' walk south on Greycliffe Avenue and then east along Wentworth Road to reach the historic **Vaucluse House** ❹ (Wentworth Road; tel: 02 9388 7922; www.hht.nsw.gov.au; Fri–Sun 9.30am–4pm; charge). A small stone cottage stood on the site as far back as 1803, but in 1827 the property was bought by William Charles Wentworth (*see margin, right*). He refurbished and extended it, and today the house, with its sweep of landscaped grounds and gardens, is one of the city's most significant historic sites.

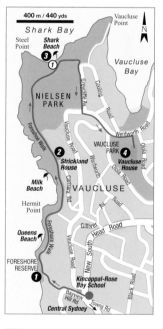

Above from far left: picturesque Shark Beach (Nielsen Park Beach); an appealing way to get around; Strickland House.

Colonial Name
William Charles Wentworth was among the most influential figures in the earliest days of the colony. He took part in the first crossing of the Blue Mountains (*see p.84*) and formed the colony's first university and independent newspaper. However, his wife, the daughter of ex-convicts, was ostracised socially for having borne two of their children out of wedlock.

Food and Drink

① **THE BEACH HOUSE**
Nielsen Park; tel: 02 9337 7333; www.nielsenpark.com.au; daily B, L, summer Fri–Sat D also; $–$$
This gorgeous listed kiosk is a year-round favourite for breakfast and lunch. Start with a baked pie of slow-cooked free range lamb shank, borlotti beans, green peas and gremolata, but leave room for one of the delicious desserts.

SOUTH HEAD AND WATSONS BAY

Guarding the entrance to Sydney Harbour, South Head has two very different sides: one wild and windswept; the other featuring sheltered coves perfect for bathing. Military buffs will love the area's rich history, while others will simply enjoy some of the best views in Sydney.

Local Flora
Most of the vegetation on South Head is heathland and scrub. Typical plants include banksias, smouldering specimens of which were used by Aboriginal tribes to transport fire from one place to another.

> **DISTANCE** 4.5km (2¾ miles)
> **TIME** A half-/full day
> **START** Macquarie Lighthouse
> **END** Hornby Lighthouse
> **POINTS TO NOTE**
> This walk can be combined with the previous one *(see p.64)*; simply catch bus no. 324 for the short trip from Shark Beach to Christison Park. Alternatively, catch this bus from town. After the tour, catch a ferry from Watsons Bay Wharf back to Circular Quay.

An easy clifftop walk starting at Christison Park leads you along first the ocean side of South Head, then the calmer harbour side. The area, formerly owned by the army, and now a national park, remains rich in military relics.

MACQUARIE LIGHTHOUSE

The most impressive building on the first section of the walk is the **Macquarie Lighthouse** ❶, Australia's oldest lighthouse. A beacon stood on this site as early as 1791. Fired by wood, it was used to guide vessels to the harbour entrance at night. In 1816, work began on a lighthouse, designed by convict architect Francis Greenway *(see p.44)*. Governor Macquarie was so pleased with his work that, on its completion in 1818, he granted Greenway a pardon and Greenway went on to design some of the colony's most important buildings.

Unfortunately, the sandstone used to build the lighthouse quickly began to erode, and the tower had to be held together with iron bands. In 1883 work commenced on a replacement, designed by James Barnet. This is the building that can be seen today, although remnants of the first lighthouse are also visible nearby.

SIGNAL STATION

Northeast of the lighthouse is the **Signal Station** ❷. In its infancy, Sydney depended heavily on supply

ships from England. For the first two years of the colony, a party of marines was sent to Botany Bay each week to see whether any ships had arrived, unaware that the settlement had moved to Port Jackson (the harbour containing Sydney Harbour, North Harbour and Middle Harbour and named by Captain James Cook, when he discovered the inlet in 1770). In 1790, a more efficient approach was adopted, and a lookout post erected on South Head.

The existing Signal Station dates back to 1842. In 1854, with the outbreak of the Crimean War, a cannon was placed below the Signal Station, to alert the colony in case a Russian fleet arrived at the heads. The adjacent gun fortifications and tunnels were added in 1892, and upgraded during World War II.

Dunbar Plaque

About 100m/yds further on is a plaque that commemorates the wreck of the *Dunbar*. In 1857, the *Dunbar*, a ship from England, was wrecked on the rocks just south of the towering headland. Of the 122 people on board, only one survived: crewman James Johnson, who was miraculously lifted by the water on to a rock ledge.

THE GAP

From here, the walk continues along the cliff's edge, past a verdant gully filled with cabbage palms, tree ferns and figs,

to **The Gap ❸**, the scenic ocean cliff that is also one of Sydney's most popular suicide spots. Recently, it played a starring role in the long-running legal case of Gordon Wood, who was accused of murdering his girlfriend, model Caroline Byrne, by pushing her off the cliff. In 2008, 13 years after Byrne's death, Wood – formerly the driver of one of Australia's most flamboyant businessmen, Rene Rivkin – was finally convicted of the crime.

Above from far left: banksias, which are typical of the vegetation in this area; Watsons Bay from above; yacht, coming into the bay.

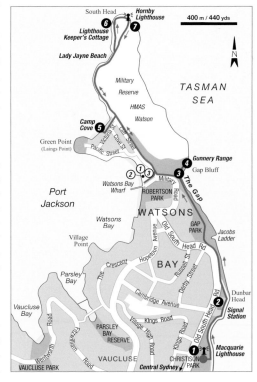

GUNNERY RANGE

About 10m/yds past The Gap, steps to the right take you to the **Gunnery Range ❹**. In 1894, four obsolete muzzle-loading 80-pounder guns were mounted here as a practice battery. A year later, the School of Gunnery was relocated from Middle Head to South Head. The gunnery was dismantled in 1917, but the parapets and the circular rails that the guns traversed are still visible.

Guns and Roses

Near the lookout is a plaque marked 'Guns and Roses', which indicates the path to Inner South Head. On the way, you will pass the remains of some of the 30 buildings that once stood here. Although the scrubby native vegetation is taking over, keen observers may spot remnants of anything from walls and tiles to bricks and fountains. The only original building still standing is the **Armoury Building**, dating back to 1838, which marks the end of the path. These days, it is used as a function centre. Behind it is the Artillery Cottage, dating back to 1895.

SANDY BEACHES

At the end of the path, turn right and follow the signs for the South Head Heritage Trail. This will bring you to **Camp Cove ❺**, a sheltered beach that is a great place for a swim. The beach has a kiosk selling cool drinks and ice creams. The Heritage Trail (at this point a cobblestone roadway), which was used to transport guns and hardware from Camp Cove Wharf to the South Head batteries, begins at the far end of the beach. The trail takes you past another popular swimming spot – **Lady Jayne Beach** – one of Sydney's three designated nudist beaches.

LIGHTHOUSE KEEPER'S COTTAGE

The wreck of the *Dunbar* (see p.67) led to the decision to build a lighthouse on South Head. Fittingly, the first lighthouse keeper to live here was none other

Invasion Fears

Although it is hard to imagine why anyone would want to attack a remote penal settlement, the threat of invasion was ever-present in colonists' minds, and led to the fortification of South Head. Just where the attacks were supposed to come from changed with the years. In the 1820s, fear of the French (England's traditional enemy) began to be replaced by fear of the US, which was growing in power. Fear reached fever pitch in 1839, when six North American ships entered the harbour by night, and were not spotted until the sun rose the next day. That led to the decision to fortify Pinchgut (now Fort Denison), Bradley's Head and South Head. In 1853, suspicion once again fell on the French, thanks to their decision to colonise the South Pacific island of New Caledonia. The next year, however, France changed its status to ally, when Britain and France joined forces against Russia in the Crimean War.

than Henry Johnson, the brother of the *Dunbar's* sole survivor. The lighthouse and the adjacent **Lighthouse Keeper's Cottage ❻** were designed by Alexander Dawson. Tragically, before the lighthouse was finished, another ship, the *Catherine Adamson*, was wrecked off North Head, on the other side of the harbour mouth, with 21 lives lost.

HORNBY LIGHTHOUSE

Further along the path you will come to the **Hornby Lighthouse ❼** itself, with its distinctive red-and-white vertical stripes. The name was chosen by the Governor, Sir William Denison, but its origin is uncertain; one theory

suggests that it was named after British Admiral Horatio Hornby, who also happened to be Lady Denison's father. Originally lit by 16 kerosene lamps, it was converted to gas in 1904, and then electrified in 1948.

Ending the Tour

After the lighthouse, the track loops around, returning you to the path. Head back to Camp Cove, then go southeast on Cliff Street to reach Robertson Park. Here you can recover with fish and chips at **Doyles**, see ⑪① and ⑪②, or the **Watsons Bay Hotel**, see ⑪③, before heading to Watsons Bay Wharf at the foot of the park, and catching a ferry back to the Circular Quay.

Above from far left: Gunnery Range; the Lightkeeper's Cottage, with the red-and-white Hornby Lighthouse behind.

Below left: Fort Denison (*see feature box, opposite*).

Food and Drink 🍴

① DOYLES ON THE BEACH
11 Marine Parade, Watsons Bay; tel: 02 9337 2007; www.doyles.com.au; daily L, D; $$$

② DOYLES ON THE WHARF
The Wharf, Watsons Bay; tel: 02 9337 6214; www.doyles.com.au; daily L, D; $$–$$$
The Doyle family have been selling seafood at Watsons Bay since 1885, and today's visitors can choose from two outlets. The more formal Doyles on the Beach has superb, if expensive, seafood platters; Doyles on the Wharf is a more casual eat-in or takeaway joint.

③ WATSONS BAY HOTEL
1 Military Road, Watsons Bay; tel: 02 9337 5444; www.watsonsbayhotel.com.au; daily L, D; $–$$
Summer weekends at the 'Watto' are a Sydney institution. Steaks, salads and fish and chips in the shady beer garden, washed down by cold 'schooners', are the perfect way to while away an afternoon. If it is hot, head to Camp Cove beach for a quick dip between courses.

BONDI AND BEYOND

Sydney's most famous beach is just the beginning; stretching south from Bondi is a chain of beaches, linked by a coastal walk that offers spectaclar ocean panoramas. This walk takes in rugged cliffs and pockets of subtropical forest, with plenty of opportunities to dive in and refresh yourself along the way.

Sharks

Bondi and its neighbouring beaches can be dangerous, with rips that carry swimmers out to sea, and occasional shark sightings. Follow basic beach rules: always swim between the flags, and if the shark alarm sounds, get out of the water at once.

DISTANCE 5.5km (3½ miles)
TIME A half-/full day
START Bondi Beach
END Coogee Beach
POINTS TO NOTE
This tour can get very crowded, particularly on fine weekends, so tackling it on a weekday is recommended. If you prefer a shorter walk, the first section, to Bronte Beach, is just 1.5km (1 mile). Stop there for a coffee before returning the way you came. Whether you are doing the whole walk or just part of it, pack your 'swimmers', water, high-factor sunscreen and a hat. To get to Bondi from town, take bus no. 380, 382 or 333 (the last is the fastest, as it is prepay only). If you are finishing the walk at Coogee, bus nos 372, 373 and 374 will take you back to town.

The residents of Sydney's posh eastern suburbs have a reputation for being pleased with themselves, and on a balmy spring day, it is not hard to see why. As you stroll or jog along the spectacular cliff walk linking no fewer than five of Sydney's favourite beaches, not to mention a couple of popular ocean baths, it is hard to think of a better way to start the day.

BONDI BEACH

Bondi Beach ❶ is perhaps Australia's most famous beach, and a source of both pride and exasperation to locals. They love the Art Deco buildings along Campbell Parade, the main road that runs alongside the beach, but hate the traffic that clogs it. They love the concerts and events held on grassy Bondi Park and in the Bondi Pavilion, but resent the crowds that come along. Most of all, however, they love the gently curving beach and the brilliant blue water that washes up against it.

Start at Notts Avenue at the south end of Bondi Beach, and walk to the end of the road, past the **Bondi Icebergs Club ❷** (1 Notts Avenue; tel: 02 9130 3120; www.icebergs.com.au; Mon–Fri 11am–late, Sat–Sun 9am–late; charge), a local icon. The baths themselves date back to the 1880s, and have been home to the Icebergs since

1929. The club's season begins in early winter, when a tonne of ice is deposited in the pool. Since a controversial redevelopment in 2001, the club is also home to one of Sydney's most glamorous venues, **Icebergs Dining Room and Bar**, see ⑪①.

Past the Icebergs, stairs take you down through the rocky cove known as **The Boot**, then back up the cliff to soak up the vista from **Mackenzie's Point**. Public toilets are available here in Marks Park. If you look carefully, you can see Aboriginal rock carvings of a shark or whale next to the path south of the point. (Whales migrate along this coast June–early July and Sept–Nov.)

TAMARAMA BEACH

Continuing around the path will bring you to **Tamarama Beach ❸**, known as Glamarama in tribute to the chic eastern-suburbs types who congregate here. Directly behind the beach is the pocket-sized **Tamarama Park**, a verdant spot that was once home to Wonderland City, Sydney's first amusement park. These days it has a cafe, toilets and play equipment, and lush subtropical vegetation. If you are planning on taking a dip, stay strictly within the flags; Tamarama is known for its dangerous rips.

BRONTE BEACH

Following the path around the next headland, you come to **Bronte Beach ❹**, named not for the family of writers but for the English Admiral Horatio Nelson, who was also the Duke of Bronte. Bronte is a favourite with eastern-suburbs families thanks to its

Above from far left: surfers on Bondi Beach; lifeguards in their distinctive shorts.

Above: swimmers at Bondi Beach beach; Bondi Icebergs Club.

Food and Drink 🍴

① ICEBERGS DINING ROOM AND BAR

1 Notts Avenue, Bondi Beach; tel: 02 9365 9000; www.idrb.com; Tue–Sun L, D; $$$

If all Icebergs had to offer was the view, it would still be worth a visit. Throw in chic interiors, attentive service, a fantastic wine list and simple yet perfectly finished Mediterranean food, and you have one of the quintessential Sydney dining experiences. For a cheaper treat, have a cocktail or two instead – just remember to 'frock up'.

Left: Bondi Beach.

Sculpture by the Sea

Each November, the Bondi to Bronte walk is home to the hugely popular Sculpture by the Sea exhibition, during which contemporary works are exhibited on land and, sometimes, floating in the ocean.

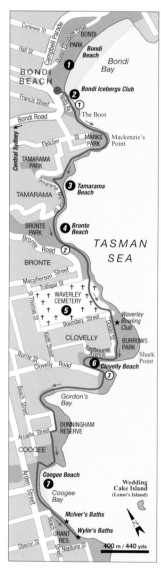

seawater baths, sprawling parklands with barbecue facilities, toilets and a little steam train for the kids. The small strip of cafes opposite the beach is a great place to relax with a coffee, if you can find a seat, that is. Try **Jenny's Cafe**, see ⑪②.

WAVERLEY CEMETERY

Cut through the car park behind the seawater baths and continue along the cliff edge to what may be the most spectacularly located cemetery in the world. The 16 hectares (40 acres) of **Waverley Cemetery** ❺ (St Thomas Street, Bronte; tel: 02 9665 4938; www.waverley.nsw.gov.au/cemetery; daily 7am–dusk; free) are home to over 50,000 burials, ranging from simple grassy plots to elaborate tombs. Among the famous Australians buried here are poets Henry Lawson and Dorothea McKellar, aviator Lawrence Hargrave, test cricketer Victor Trumper and champion swimmer Fanny Durack.

CLOVELLY BEACH

Once you come out of the cemetery, follow the path past Clovelly Bowling Club to come to **Clovelly Beach** ❻. At the bottom of a long, narrow bay, lying between two rocky ridges and protected by a breakwater, the beach's calm waters make it a favourite with families. Snorkellers also head here to

check out the local marine life, and concrete platforms on both sides of the bay are popular places for sunbathers, with a small pool set into the western side beneath the surf lifesaving club, where there is also a good cafe, **Seasalt**, see .

COOGEE BEACH

From the surf lifesaving club, cut through the car park to rejoin the walk at Gordon's Bay, where the rocks are another popular spot for sunbathers and swimmers. A steep run of stairs makes this the most tiring section of the walk, but once around the bay, you emerge onto the bare headland of Coogee. From here you can either walk down to **Coogee Beach ❼**, or continue past it to two popular baths on the rock platforms located just south of the beach.

Coogee's Saltwater Baths

The first one you come to, **McIver's Baths** (Grant Reserve, Beach Street; daily sunrise to sunset; charge), is better known as the Women's Baths. The secluded 20m/yd ocean pool set on a rock platform has been used solely by women and children since the late 1800s. For a nominal entry fee, women can relax in a secluded, well-screened space. Its counterpart, the men-only Giles Baths, was closed in the 1970s after suffering severe storm damage.

Further along the walk are **Wylie's Baths** (Grant Reserve, Beach Street; tel: 02 9665 2838; daily: Oct–early Apr 7am–7pm, early Apr–Sept 7am–5pm; charge), built in 1907 by champion swimmer Henry Alexander Wylie. The baths were one of the first mixed-gender bathing pools in Australia, and were used by Wylie's daughter Wilhelmina, who, along with Fanny Durack, was one of Australia's first two female Olympic swimmers. The baths have a 45m/yd pool with a sweeping 180-degree view, and also offer yoga classes.

Above from far left: artworks set out for Sculpture by the Sea (see opposite); Coogee Beach; more Sculpture by the Sea; Bronte Beach.

Food and Drink 🍴

② JENNY'S CAFE
485 Bronte Road, Bronte; tel: 02 9389 7498; daily B, L, AT; $
Few Sydney cafes are as busy as the small venues squashed next to each other opposite Bronte Beach. Jenny's Cafe has a relaxed, homely feel, as well as an array of freshly pressed juices, cakes and coffee.

③ SEASALT
1 Donnellan Circuit, Clovelly; tel: 02 9664 5344; www.seasaltcafe.com.au; daily B, L; $–$$
It may be less glamorous than Bondi or Bronte, but Clovelly has at least one chic cafe that can compete with its neighbours. Tucked below the lifesaving club, Seasalt has an interior designed by the acclaimed team of Burley Katon Halliday, and serves salads, sandwiches, pasta and seafood.

BOTANY BAY

This tour travels to the birthplace of European Australia – the bay where Captain Cook anchored over 200 years ago, so starting a new chapter in the continent's history. Bush walks, picnics and monuments are all part of this historic day trip.

DISTANCE 65km (40 miles)
TIME A full day
START/END Sydney
POINTS TO NOTE
You will need a car to do this complete tour, which takes in two headlands at either side of Botany Bay, but if you are short of time, or you do not want to drive, you can take a direct bus (no. 394 from Circular Quay) to La Perouse. If you are going to La Perouse, try to do so on a Sunday, when the fort is open and the snake show (*see p.76*) is on. The distance above shows the full route (including to Kurnell), marked in red on the map.

Botany Bay is where the European history of Australia began. At 3pm on 29 April 1770, Captain James Cook stepped ashore from the *Endeavour* to claim the 'Great South Land' for Britain. The anchorage was named Botany Bay after more than 3,000 new botanical specimens were collected by the expedition's naturalist, Joseph Banks, during the eight days the ship was moored here. In 1788, the First Fleet also stopped off briefly but, finding the site unsuitable for a permanent settlement, moved on to Sydney Cove. The name Botany Bay became 19th-century shorthand for the terrors that awaited convicts transported down under.

TOWARDS BOTANY BAY

Allow about an hour for the drive to Kurnell. Head south from Sydney on the Eastern Distributor. Turn left onto General Holmes Drive and follow the signs to Rockdale. Turn right onto President Avenue to join Princes Highway. At Kogarah, take Rocky Point Road, following the sign for Ramsgate and Cronulla, and cross the Georges River to Taren Point. Turn left at Captain Cook Drive, following the sign for **Kurnell**. From here, it's another 10km (6 miles) until you arrive at **Botany Bay National Park**. You can drive into the park (a fee applies), or park on the street outside.

The drive is not a particularly scenic one, winding through red-roofed suburbs to the Kurnell Peninsula. Many of Sydney's most unloved projects –

Above from left:
Captain Cook taking possession of New South Wales in 1770 in the name of the British crown; dedicated track on Botany Bay.

from huge oil refineries to a desalination plant – end up here. However, Botany Bay National Park – 436 hectares (1,000 acres) of coastal cliffs, heath, woodland and quiet beaches – remains a popular destination for weekend picnics, and plenty of swimmers are happy to plunge into the water within sight of the refineries.

CAPTAIN COOK'S LANDING SITE

Head down to the water to join the **Monument Track ❶**, a 1km (¼-mile) wheelchair-accessible walk along the coast to the park's visitor centre. On the way you pass monuments including the Captain Cook Obelisk (1870), the Sir Joseph Banks Memorial (1947), the Solander Monument (1914) and a memorial to Seaman Forby Sutherland, the first European known to be buried on the continent. The **Discovery Centre ❷** (Botany Bay National Park, Cape Solander Drive; tel: 02 9668 2000; daily 9.30am–4.30pm) is the place to pick up park maps, and also has toilet facilities and a canteen selling ice creams and snacks.

Bush Walks

Several walks start on the far side of the centre's car park, including the 1km (¼-mile) **Yena Track**. The track is marked with signs about local flora, including how the local Gwyeagal

people used plants such as the wattle: its fibre for utensils, its leaves as fish poison, its unripe seeds as soap and its ripe roasted seeds as fuel. Particularly on a hot day, when the cicadas are shrilling

Below: Captain Cook Obelisk.

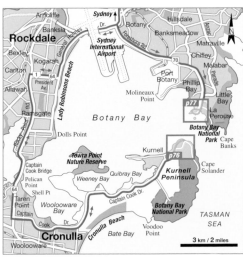

Snake-Charming
Every Sunday afternoon from 1.30pm, a burly snake-charmer shows off his reptilian mates near the last bus stop at La Perouse, a tradition that was started in the 1920s.

and kookaburras calling, walking past the Scribbly Gums and through the heath, it is easy to imagine how strange this landscape must have seemed to the newly arrived Europeans.

The Yena Track leads to a scenic coastal outlook, from where you can either return to the Discovery Centre via the **Mauru Track**, or continue along the clifftop to join the **Cape Baily Coast Walk**, an 8km (5-mile) stroll past dunes, heathlands and swamps. The views are magnificent, and in June and early July and from September to November, you may even spot migrating whales.

LA PEROUSE

From Kurnell, you can either return to the city the way you came, or take a detour to **La Perouse**. Head back towards the airport, and follow the signs to the right for Port Botany. These will take you onto Foreshore Road, past ranks of container storage. Turn right at Bunnerong Road (which joins Anzac Parade just before the

peninsula) and follow the road until you reach La Perouse, where beaches, bushland, historic buildings and fish-and-chips shops are jumbled together at the end of the peninsula. The loop road on the headland was originally a circular track forming part of the tram terminus, before the trams were de-commissioned in 1961.

The French Fleet

The suburb is named after the Comte de La Pérouse, the French naval commander who arrived in Botany Bay just eight days after Captain Phillip and the First Fleet in 1788. The meeting was cordial enough, though the British were unable to assist the French with food, as they were running short themselves. La Pérouse set up a camp on the north shore, and when he left, entrusted his journals and letters to the British ship *Sirius*, which was returning to Europe. This was a fortunate move, as his ships disappeared after departing Botany Bay for New Caledonia; the wrecks were only discovered in 1964.

Historic Buildings

The round tower at the start of the loop is the **Macquarie Watchtower ❸**, constructed in the 1820s to house a small squad of soldiers stationed on the point to prevent smuggling. At the bottom of the loop lies **Bare Island ❹** (tel: 02 9311 3379; charge), which got its name from Captain Cook's description of it as 'a small bare island'.

Map:
300 m / 330 yds
Sutherland Point
Inscription Point
Seaman Forby Sutherland
Solander Monument
Botany Bay
Silver Beach
Monument Track
❶
❷
i Discovery Centre
Cook Obelisk
Muru Track
Charles Pde
Captain Cook Dr
Polo Street
Botany Bay National Park
Yena Track
Cape Baily
Cardin Cook
Cook St
KURNELL

The island, now linked to the mainland by a footbridge, was fortified in 1885, with fortifications designed by colonial architect James Barnet. For 50 years it was used as a retirement home for war veterans, until it was handed over to the New South Wales Parks and Wildlife Service in 1963. Tours take place on Sundays at 1.30pm, 2.30pm and 3.30pm. Tickets can be bought from the La Perouse Museum a little further around the loop.

La Perouse Museum

The building housing the **La Perouse Museum** ❺ (tel: 02 9311 3379; Wed–Sun 10am–4pm; charge) was built in 1882 as a cable station and housed workers operating the 1876 undersea telegraph line to New Zealand. It now contains maps, scientific instruments and relics linked to the French explorers.

Near the museum is the **La Perouse Monument**, an obelisk erected in 1825 by the French, and a memorial marking the grave of one of the expedition's scientists, Father Receveur.

HENRY HEAD TRACK

From here, treat yourself to some fish and chips from **Danny's Seafood**, see ❶①, or, if you are still feeling energetic, take the signposted 5km (3-mile) walk along the **Henry Head Track** from La Perouse Museum to the Endeavour Lighthouse. The track passes through coastal heath, angophora forest and mil-

itary fortifications. From the lighthouse, there are fine views across the bay.

Along the walk, information signs explain the history of the area, including the squatters' camp that housed at least 330 people during the 1930s depression. Camps such as this one were found on coastal land around Sydney, with huts built out of whatever material was available, such as corrugated iron, hessian and earth.

To return to Sydney city centre, head north on Anzac Parade via Kingsford.

Above from far left: tranquil Botany Bay; Bare Island.

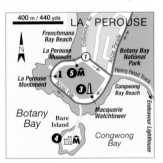

Food and Drink

① **DANNY'S SEAFOOD**
1605 Anzac Parade, La Perouse; tel: 02 9311 4116; www.dannys. net.au; daily L, D; $–$$
Danny's has been serving up seafood by the beach for approximately 30 years. Downstairs, the chefs dole out straightforward fish and chips – eat at one of the outside tables, or take it with you to the beach – while upstairs, you will be offered a more sophisticated seafood experience.

THE SPIT TO MANLY

In a city blessed with an abundance of fabulous foreshore walks, the Spit to Manly walk is the most magnificent of all. The trail through swathes of untouched bushland offers magnificent harbour panoramas and secluded beaches, and culminates in one of Sydney's favourite seaside playgrounds.

Paddling Around
The calm waters between The Spit and Manly are perfect for kayaking, and there are several local outfits offering kayak hire and kayak tours. On the eastern side of the Spit Bridge, right under Harry's Fish Cafe, is Sydney Harbour Kayaks (tel: 02 9960 4389; www.sydneyharbour kayaks.com.au). On the Manly side, Manly Kayaks is located next to Oceanworld (tel: 1800 KAYAKS; www.manlykayaks. com.au).

DISTANCE 9.25km (5¾ miles)
TIME A full day
START Ellery's Punt Reserve
END Shelly Beach
POINTS TO NOTE
This foreshore walk is strenuous, involving rough tracks and lots of stairs. There are no refreshments available en route, so be sure to pack some water and snacks along with your swimsuit, hat and sunscreen. To get to the starting point, you can either catch a bus from Wynyard station (suitable routes include the 140 and 190; for more information, visit www. 131500.com.au or call 131 500), or catch a taxi. From Manly, catch a ferry back to the city.

This tour on the northern side of the Middle Harbour offers an insight into two very different aspects of how Sydneysiders make use of their harbour. The foreshore walk takes you through a landscape that in parts is unchanged from the time of the arrival of the Europeans. However,

Manly, the seaside suburb famously 'seven miles from Sydney, a thousand miles from care', has long been a place for locals to escape the hustle and bustle of the big smoke. Allow about three hours for the foreshore walk, and a few extra hours for exploring what Manly has to offer.

ELLERY'S PUNT RESERVE

Ask your bus driver or taxi driver to drop you at the southern end of Spit Bridge, and take the walkway on the western side of the bridge. At the far end there is a staircase leading down to a grassy clearing and popular fishing spot called **Ellery's Punt Reserve ❶**. In the 1850s, before the construction of the first bridge in 1924, Manly was connected to The Spit by a punt that carried pedestrians and horse, tram and vehicular traffic. The tram service ceased in 1939, but the walkway follows the old tram route for 200m/yds towards Fishers Bay, where subtropical rainforest vegetation can be seen along the banks of the creek that runs into the bay.

CLONTARF BEACH

A 20-minute walk will bring you to **Clontarf Beach ❷**, a family-friendly spot with picnic shelters, toilets and other facilities. Clontarf's moment of fame came in 1868, when it was the site of an assassination attempt on Queen Victoria's second son, Prince Alfred *(see margin, p.46)*. The bullet was deflected by the prince's rubber braces. Stairs at the far end of Clontarf Beach, which take you up to the path, may be inaccessible at high tide. An alternative route, via Monash Crescent, is clearly marked.

GROTTO POINT

The next hour of the walk is the most strenuous, with the path winding up and down hills and frequent stairs. If you need to cool off, there are steps down to tiny **Castle Rock Beach ❸**. Alter- natively, continue along the path to **Grotto Point**, where a First Fleet survey party camped in January 1788. A sign- post shows you the way to the **Grotto Point lighthouse**, a 1km (³/₄-mile) detour. The building, which resembles a Greek chapel, was built in 1911 and is still used to guide ships entering the har- bour. Return to the path and, after a short while, you will come to a clearing on your right that contains a number of clearly marked Aboriginal carvings.

FORTY BASKETS BEACH

After continuing uphill again, the path takes a detour through a number of suburban streets, including Ogilvy Road, Vista Avenue and Bareena Drive, before coming to **Tania Park**, named after one of the area's first local celebrities, Tania Verstak, who was crowned Miss Australia in 1961 and Miss International Beauty in 1962.

Above from far left: Manly; Clontarf Beach.

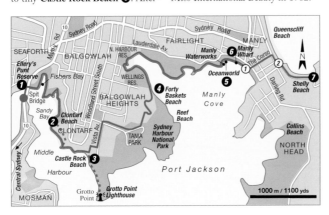

Above from left:
Shelly Beach; Palm Beach *(see p.83)*.

On the far side of the park, follow the signs to descend to **Forty Baskets Beach** ❹, a name commemorating a catch of 40 baskets of fish that were sent to Sudanese troops encamped at the North Head Quarantine Station in 1885. You have now re-entered suburbia, travelling through Wellings Reserve and North Harbour Reserve, where there are picnic facilities and playgrounds. Continue along the opposite side of the cove to Fairlight Beach; the path from here around to Manly is very popular, due to its gentle slope.

OCEANWORLD

Once you round the corner into Manly Cove, you come to **Oceanworld** ❺ (West Esplanade; tel: 02 8251 7877;

daily 10am–5.30pm; charge), a 4 million-litre (880,000-gallon) aquarium. Along with the touch pools and main tank, there are sessions featuring Australia's most dangerous animals, including snakes, spiders and crocodiles. Oceanworld's biggest attraction, however, is the opportunity to dive with sharks, for which bookings are essential. Right next door is **Manly Waterworks**, a playpark with giant slides that is very popular with children.

MANLY

Two hundred metres/yds along from Oceanworld is **Manly Wharf** ❻. This is where the ferry from Circular Quay pulls in and also something of an entertainment hub, with pubs and restaurants. Grab a bite at one of the restaurants lining The Esplanade, such as **Out of Africa**, see ①①, or head down The Corso, a lively pedestrian zone that continues all the way to the surf side of Manly. At Manly, Norfolk pines line the long stretch of beach (Queenscliff Beach to your left and Manly Cove to your right). Here again, there are plenty of eateries, such as **Whitewater**, see ①②, lining the street opposite the beach.

Head right for another short scenic walk along Manly Cove to the peaceful **Shelly Beach** ❼. When you are ready, stroll back along The Corso to Manly Wharf, and hop on a ferry back to Circular Quay.

Food and Drink

① OUT OF AFRICA

43–5 East Esplanade, Manly; tel: 02 9977 0055; www.out ofafrica.com.au; Thur–Sun L, D, Mon–Wed D; $–$$
The orange walls and zebra-striped banquette of this long-time favourite are eye-catching, but the food is equally as attention-grabbing. Moroccan tagines are the speciality of the house, but the menu includes many dishes from across the continent, including South African *sosaties* (kebabs).

② WHITEWATER

35 South Steyne, Manly; tel: 02 9977 0322; www.whitewater restaurant.com.au; Sat–Sun B, L, D, Mon–Fri L, D; $–$$
It's been a long time since Manly's culinary offerings were limited to fish and chips. These days, the area has many sophisticated diners like this one, with its bluestone feature wall and white leather banquettes. Seafood is a specialty, from fresh oysters to hiramasa kingfish and whitebait fritters.

NORTHERN BEACHES

Known to locals as The Peninsula, the Northern Beaches are among the city's most exclusive addresses. Characterised by sweeping beaches, palm trees, chic cafes and expensive homes, this is one of Sydneysiders' favourite summer haunts.

Northern Beaches' residents like to think of themselves as being a breed apart, and when you drive up there, it is not hard to see why – The Peninsula does feel like a different world.

Take the Northbridge exit from the Harbour Bridge (after the North Sydney exit) and follow the signs to Northbridge and then on to the Eastern Valley Way all the way through **Forestville**. Twenty metres/yds after the Forest High School, turn left onto the Wakehurst Parkway, one of Sydney's most attractive roads. For about 10km (6 miles) it cuts straight through dense bushland, emerging at the other end at the peaceful **Narrabeen Lakes**. The road ends in a T-junction; turn left onto Pittwater Road and head towards Mona Vale shops, about 6km (4 miles) away.

DISTANCE 20km (12½ miles)
TIME A full day
START Bungan Beach
END Palm Beach
POINTS TO NOTE
The L90 bus runs from the city to Palm Beach but, depending on traffic, the trip can take up to two hours. The best way to explore the Northern Beaches is definitely by car, although you will need to have lots of coins for the parking meters. Remember to pack your swimsuit, hat and sun cream.

BUNGAN BEACH

When you reach the shopping centre, veer left onto Barrenjoey Road as it climbs the headland overlooking **Newport Beach**. At the crest of the hill, turn right at Karlo Parade, then right into Bungan Road and park, if you can, on the corner of Myola Road. A long, steep hill descends to **Bungan Beach ❶**, one of Sydney's most secluded beaches. On weekdays, it feels like your own personal beach, with perhaps just a handful of surfers sharing the water with you.

Returning the way you came, turn right onto Barrenjoey Road and then left into Beaconsfield Street, following the road all the way down to The Peninsula's favourite pub. Set on the shores of Pittwater, **The Newport Arms Hotel**, see ❶① *(see p.82)*, opened in 1880 and today has the Northern Beaches' largest outdoor screen, on which sporting events are shown.

Summer Bay
To millions of UK viewers, Palm Beach is better known as Summer Bay. The beach is where the outdoor scenes of the popular series *Home and Away* are filmed.

BILGOLA BEACH

From the Newport Arms, it is not far to another of The Peninsula's hidden beaches. **Bilgola Beach ❷** is nestled deep between high headlands in a small, subtropical rainforest of ferns and exotic blooms. To get there, return to Barrenjoey Road and keep heading north, turning right at The Serpentine. The parking lot for Bilgola is the first right turn at the bottom of the hill. The beach has a kiosk selling basic refreshments.

AVALON

As you leave the beach, turn right into The Serpentine, which is as winding as the name suggests, and wend your way back to Barrenjoey Road. Turning right at the next traffic lights will bring you to Avalon, the liveliest place on The Peninsula. Park where you can, then stroll down **Old Barrenjoey Road ❸**, home to a range of chic cafes and boutiques, including **The Cook's Larder**, see ⑪②, and a fine bookstore/café, **Bookoccino**.

Food and Drink 🍴

① THE NEWPORT ARMS HOTEL
Corner of Beaconsfield and Kalinya streets, Newport; tel: 02 9997 4900; www.newportarms.com.au; Mon–Sat 10am–midnight, Sun 10am–10pm; $$–$$$
This pub has the largest beer garden in Australia, a green family-friendly space that is a great place to grab a burger or some grilled seafood, or simply chill out for an afternoon.

② THE COOK'S LARDER
21–3 Old Barrenjoey Road, Avalon; tel: 02 9973 4370; www.thecookslarder.com.au; daily B, L, Thur–Sat D; $–$$
A homely outlet that combines a delicatessen and cafe, with tables scattered along the footpath. Its homemade cakes are what really draw the crowds, but if you feel like something more hardy, a well-executed risotto or poached salmon are the types of dishes on offer.

③ JONAH'S
69 Bynya Road, Palm Beach; tel: 02 9974 5599; www.jonahs.com.au; summer daily B, L, D, winter Wed–Sun D; $$$
A meal at Jonah's has long been a way to seal the deal on a new romance, not least because of the luxurious hotel rooms attached to the restaurant. The view is one of the best in Sydney, and the menu, slanted towards seafood, is also impressive.

④ BEACH ROAD
1 Beach Road, Palm Beach; tel: 02 9974 1159; www.beachroad.com.au; Sat–Sun L, Fri–Sat D; $$$$
Located in a sunny spot opposite the grassy headland, Beach Road has shaded tables, live music on Sunday afternoons and a menu that ranges from scallops and Yamba prawns served with chorizo and hot buttered spinach, to grain-fed Angus beef with mushrooms.

PALM BEACH

Keep heading north on Barrenjoey Road past Whale Beach (the location of the renowned, and wonderfully romantic, **Jonah's**, see 🍴③), to **Palm Beach ❹**, the area's most prestigious address. There are actually two beaches here, separated by Barrenjoey Headland. The surf beach on the right is Palm Beach proper; from the far end of the more tranquil bayside beach on the left, you can access one of two tracks that lead to the **Barrenjoey Lighthouse**, perched 113m (371ft) above Broken Bay. Both are steep, but the left-hand path is much easier than the right-hand path. Allow about an hour for the return journey.

THE BASIN

For something to eat at this point, stop at **Beach Road**, see 🍴④, then, from the wharf on the Pittwater side of Palm Beach, you can hop on a ferry operated by the Palm Beach Ferry Service (tel: 02 9974 2411; www.palm beachferry.com.au) for a trip across Pittwater and Broken Bay.

Alight at West Head and take the walking track to the **The Basin**, in the Ku-ring-gai Chase National Park. The Basin's collection of Aboriginal art is probably the most extensive on show in the Sydney area, and was created by the Gurringgai people who occupied this territory for over 20,000 years.

Back to Sydney

To return to Sydney, take the ferry back to Palm Beach, then head back to the city centre via Pittwater Road and the Wakehurst Parkway.

Above from far left: the beach at Avalon; The Basin.

Basin Trip
The ferry ride takes 20 minutes each way, and ferries arrive/ leave every hour, so make sure you put enough money in the parking meter at Palm Beach.

BLUE MOUNTAINS

An expansive World Heritage-listed wilderness filled with deep gorges, plunging waterfalls and untouched bush, the Blue Mountains is one of NSW's most spectacular landscapes. It can be done as a long day trip from Sydney, but two days will let you take in more of the area's highlights.

DISTANCE 175km (109 miles)

TIME Two days

START/END Sydney

POINTS TO NOTE

It is possible to catch a train to Katoomba and the main villages, but to explore the area fully, you will need a car. The mountains are considerably cooler than Sydney, so take sufficient layers with you. No visit to the mountains is complete without a bush walk. A couple of short, easy options are included in the tour; if you want something more challenging, you can obtain more information from the Blue Mountains Visitor Centre at Echo Point. The distance above is for the red tour marked on the map.

Local Wildlife
The Blue Mountains World Heritage Area is home to around 400 species of birds, reptiles and mammals, 40 of which are listed as rare or endangered.

Before Sydneysiders discovered the beach, they went to the mountains. In the 1920s, the city's well-to-do retreated from the scorching city summers to the cool mountain air, creating a series of attractive townships full of guesthouses and cafes serving classic Devonshire teas. Today's visitors tend to be more adventurous, exploring the pockets of rainforest, ferns and hanging swamps, as well as the vast forests of eucalypts, which launch their oil into the air, giving the mountains their eponymous haze.

Physical Geography

The mountains here are not particularly high; Mount Victoria, the highest point, is a mere 1,111m (3,645ft) above sea level. However, the terrain is so rugged that it can hide a species of tree (the Wollemi pine) that was thought to have been extinct for 150 million years before it was recently rediscovered.

Crossing the mountains to access the pasture lands on the western side was one of the greatest challenges facing the early colonists. Indigenous tribes had of course been crossing from inland to the coast for thousands of years, but since no one thought to ask them for advice, it was not until 1813 that explorers Blaxland, Lawson and Wentworth managed the feat. Today's Great Western Highway closely follows the route they took, as does the railway that provides easy access between the city and the mountains for a growing number of commuters.

LEAVING SYDNEY

The Blue Mountains may be one of Sydney's most scenic destinations, but the drive there is anything but. To reach the Great Western Highway that takes you up to the mountains, head west on Parramatta Road from the city centre, then follow the signs.

Depending on traffic, it will take you about 90 minutes to clear the urban sprawl and start heading up through the lower mountains townships such as Springwood and Faulconbridge, where the scenery slowly starts to change to classic wooded mountain landscape.

NORMAN LINDSAY GALLERY AND MUSEUM

If you feel you need to stretch your legs before you reach Wentworth Falls *(see right)*, you can stop at Faulconbridge to visit the **Norman Lindsay Gallery and Museum ①** (14 Norman Lindsay Crescent; tel: 02 4751 1067; www. normanlindsay.com.au; daily 10am–4pm; charge), erstwhile home of one of Australia's most notorious artists, who is as famous for his Bacchanalian nudes as he is for his much-loved children's book, *The Magic Pudding*. To reach the gallery, turn right from the Great Western Highway into Grose Road, and follow the signs.

Set in beautifully landscaped gardens, the stone cottage in which Lindsay lived for 57 years, until his

death in 1969, now houses a major collection of his work. The 16 hectares (40 acres) of elaborate gardens include some of his larger statues and fountains, and his studio is set up as if he had just stepped out for a minute.

WENTWORTH FALLS

Return to the Great Western Highways and continue towards the mountains. Especially if you did not stop at the gallery, by the time you reach the township of **Wentworth Falls ②**, you will be ready for a break. Either turn right into Station Street as you come into town and stop at **Conditorei Patisserie Schwarz**, see ① ① *(see p.87)*, or stay on the Great Western Highway and take the next

Above from far left: Australian cockatoo in the Blue Mountains; bird's-eye view of the spectacular range; Wentworth Falls.

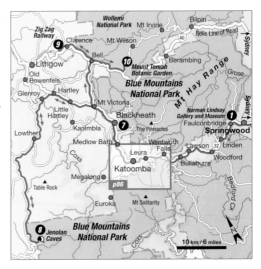

Summer Yule

Winter in the Blue Mountains can be a decidedly chilly affair, by Sydney standards at least. The regular heavy fogs and occasional flurries of snow appeal to locals who head here to celebrate Yulefest – Christmas in July – complete with a traditional English Christmas dinner.

left at Falls Road (look for the sign to Wentworth Falls National Park). Fletcher Street is the third cross street; turn right at the sign for **The Conservation Hut**, see ⑪②. The hut is at the end of the street; from here, you can access a variety of viewpoints, including Princes Rock Lookout, which gives a good view of Wentworth Falls. The mountains' best waterfall is impressive when it is in full flood; during dry periods it slows to a trickle.

LEURA

Head back to the Great Western Highway and continue on to **Leura** ❸, one of the prettiest villages in the mountains. Its main street, The Mall, is peppered with craft, antiques and tea shops and has one of the area's best restaurants, **Silk's Brasserie**, see ⑪③.

Also on The Mall is **Café Madeleine**, see ⑪④ – perfect if all you really want is a delicious slice of cake.

Green-fingered visitors will love **Everglades Gardens** (37 Everglades Avenue, Leura; tel: 02 4784 1938; www.everglades.org.au; spring and summer daily 10am–5pm, autumn and winter 10am–4pm; charge), which features 5 hectares (12 acres) of landscaped grounds. To get there from Leura Mall, turn left into Craigend Street, then right into Everglades Avenue.

ECHO POINT

Keep driving down The Mall and follow the scenic clifftop drive to Katoomba. On the way you will pass **Solitary Restaurant and Kiosk**, see ⑪⑤. Stop at **Echo Point** ❹, where a lookout provides a magnificent view over the famous **Three Sisters** rock formation and into the Jamison Valley. There is also a **Blue Mountains Visitor Centre** (daily 9am–5pm; tel: 1300 653 408) located here.

Scenic World

Several bush walks are accessible from Echo Point; take the **Giants Stairway** to the left of the Three Sisters that descends 1,000 steps to the valley floor, from where walks of varying length and difficulty begin. Turn right to take an easy two-hour walk to the **Scenic Railway**, part of **Scenic World** ❺ (Top Station, corner of Violet Street

and Cliff Drive, Katoomba; tel: 02 4782 2699; www.scenicworld.com.au; daily 9am–5pm; charge). Originally constructed in the 1880s to transport miners and coal up from the valley, it is the steepest railway incline in the world, and the swift ride up a sheer cliff face at a 45-degree angle can be nerve-racking. If it is any consolation, the ride back down is even more so, giving the sensation of plunging 445m (1,460ft) to the valley floor.

Alternatively, return to Katoomba via the **Scenic Cableway**, which makes the steep trip to the clifftop. There you will also find the **Scenic World Skyway**, a

Above from far left: waterfall near Leura; three women looking at the peaks of the Three Sisters.

Food and Drink

① CONDITOREI PATISSERIE SCHWARZ
30 Station Street, Wentworth Falls; tel: 02 4757 3300; daily B, L, AT; $
There is always a crush in this cafe, with queues both for tables or just to pick up some treats to go. Stock up on terrific rye and sourdough breads, or authentic German cakes such as poppyseed strudel. They also offer picnic packs for bush walkers.

② THE CONSERVATION HUT
Fletcher Street, Wentworth Falls; tel: 02 4757 3827; www.conservationhut.com.au; winter daily B, L, summer Mon–Thur B, L, Fri–Sun B, L, D; $$
Whether on the terrace in summer or by the log fire in winter, this is a great place to soak up the stunning view while enjoying a hearty meal. Lunch options range from the simple (steak sandwiches, homemade pies, etc) to the more elaborate (pan-roasted chicken with bacon, mustard braised leeks and an onion reduction, for example).

③ SILK'S BRASSERIE
128 The Mall, Leura; tel: 02 4784 2534; www.silksleura.com; daily L, D; $$–$$$
One of the mountains' most enduring dining institutions does high-class food without attitude. Occasional Asian touches enliven more traditional offerings such as pan-fried snapper served with turned potato, Dutch carrot, leek and celery paysanne, pancetta, and saffron mussel chowder sauce.

④ CAFÉ MADELEINE
187a The Mall, Leura; tel: 02 4784 3833; www.josophans.com.au; daily B, L; $
You could order eggs benedict or a smoked salmon bagel, but that alone might be a waste. Chocolate cakes are the specialty here, and treats such as Mexican chocolate cake or a white chocolate cheesecake are indulgences of the highest order.

⑤ SOLITARY RESTAURANT AND KIOSK
90 Cliff Drive, Leura Falls; tel: 02 4782 1164; www.solitary.com.au; kiosk: daily L, AT; restaurant: daily L, Sat D; $–$$$
A weatherboard cottage with panoramic views of the Jamison Valley, Solitary offers two separate dining experiences. The kiosk delivers good-value breakfasts, lunches and afternoon teas, while the fine-dining restaurant offers weekend lunches as well as dinners. Restaurant bookings essential.

glass-floored cable car that takes a 720m/yd trip across the Jamison Valley, offering unbeatable views.

KATOOMBA

From here, depending on where you have left your car, you can head into the township of **Katoomba** ❻ by taking bus no. 686 from the stop outside Scenic World. Katoomba has a slightly scruffy air, but Katoomba Street has some interesting antiques and new-age

Below: the colourful Campbell Rhododendron Garden.

shops to browse. Treat yourself to a hot drink in Katoomba's **Cafe Paragon**, see ⑪⑥, which is preserved-in-amber, before strolling back to Echo Point to pick up the car. If you are need of greater refreshment at this point, visit the highly rated **Darley's**, see ⑪⑦.

BLACKHEATH

If you are still feeling energetic, you can explore the next township, **Blackheath** ❼, before checking into your hotel. Originally called Hounslow, this settlement was a favourite stopping place for 19th-century miners heading west to dig for gold. It was renamed by Governor Macquarie in 1815 because of its black, wild look.

Campbell Rhododendron Gardens and Bush Walk

The **Campbell Rhododendron Gardens** (Bacchante Street, Blackheath; tel: 02 4787 6983; www.rhodogarden.org. au; daily 9am–4pm; charge) feature more than 1,500 rhododendrons in a bush setting, and are spectacular from September to November.

There is also a breathtaking **bush walk** from Govett's Leap lookout to Pulpit Rock, which offers an awe-inspiring panorama. The walk is about 6km (4 miles), but there is an easy option: it is just 400m/yds from the car park to the three-level Pulpit Rock lookout, which has a 240-degree view into Govett's Gorge and the Grose Valley.

This should bring you to the end of the first day. Options for staying overnight in Leura include **Broomelea Bed and Breakfast** *(see p.113)* and in Katoomba, **Echoes** and **Lialianfels** *(see p.113)*, home to Darley's *(see below)*.

JENOLAN CAVES

The next morning, take the Great Western Highway past Mount Victoria and the Victoria Pass. Just after the village of Hartley, the turnoff for Jenolan Caves is on your left. Follow the road all the way to **Jenolan Caves** (Jenolan Caves Road, Jenolan; tel: 1300 763 311; www.jenolancaves.org. au; daily 9.30am–5.30pm; charge). The drive will take about an hour; the last section of the road is very narrow, and must be tackled slowly. Jenolan Caves is a mighty series of underground limestone halls encrusted with archways, stalactites, stalagmites and underground rivers. Eleven of the caves are open to the public.

The caves, known to the Aborigines as Binoomea, or 'dark places', were officially discovered by local farmer James Whalan in 1838. Legend has it that the caves had previously been used as a hideout by outlaw James McKeown, a former convict.

Early Finds
The first cave, the Elder Cave, was explored in 1848, but it was not until 1860 that the Lucas Cave, the largest of the show caves, was discovered. In 1866, the caves were brought under government control, and in 1884 the name Jenolan Caves (from the Aboriginal word meaning 'high mountain') was given to the complex that had previously been known as the Binda ('fish river') Caves.

Many of the most spectacular caves, including the River, Temple of Baal, Orient, Ribbon and Pool of Cerberus caves, were discovered during the first years of the 20th century, when

---

Food and Drink

⑥ CAFE PARAGON
63–7 Katoomba Street, Katoomba; tel: 02 4782 2928; Sun–Fri B, L, Sat B, L, D; $–$$
The mountain air is often chilly; if you feel the need to warm up with a cuppa, head straight for the Paragon, where the gorgeous 1930s Art Deco interior has been listed by the National Trust. They also do a killer hot chocolate.

⑦ DARLEY'S
Lilianfels Blue Mountains Resort & Spa, Echo Point, Katoomba; tel: 02 4780 1200; www.lilianfels.com. au; Mon–Sat D; $$$
Hands-down the best meals available in the mountains, but expect to pay for the privilege. Tucked into a historic residence, the small rooms make for an intimate dining experience – all the better to savour the sophisticated, seasonal modern Australian cuisine. Reserve.

Above: Scenic World's Skyway cable car and gondola.

Outdoor Pursuits
The mountains' rugged landscape makes it the perfect destination for thrill seekers. Abseiling, canyoning, rock climbing and mountain biking are all popular activities, and offer a unique way to experience this wilderness. Reputable companies include High n Wild Mountain Adventures (tel: 02 4782 6224; www.high-n-wild. com.au).

Every day between 11.45am and 1.15pm, the last section of the Jenolan Valley Road becomes one-way, to allow coaches to travel safely on the narrow road. That means these hours are also peak visiting time. Plan your visit for early in the day. If necessary, there is an alternate route from the caves, via the Oberon Road.

explorations were still done by candlelight. These days the caves are electrified, and some feature sound-and-light shows. Much of the cave system, which is estimated to extend around 40km (25 miles), remains to be explored; recent discoveries include the Barralong Cave in 1963 and the Spider Cave in 1975.

Cave Tours

Tickets for each cave are sold separately, with tours departing every half an hour, occasionally more frequently. Cave tours generally last around 90 minutes, and discounts apply if you visit more than one cave. Among the most popular caves are the Pool of Cerberus Cave and the River Cave –

Right: Jenolan Caves.

Above from far left:
Mount Toombah
Botanic Gardens;
Zig Zag Railway.

the latter known for its magnificent formations, including spectacular shawls (limestone formations that hang from a cave's ceiling), stalacmites and columns. The Orient Cave is among the most beautiful, containing three richly coloured chambers, the first of which is wheelchair-accessible. The Imperial Cave is good for the less mobile, and contains the bones of a wallaby and a Tasmanian devil (long extinct on the mainland).

Adventure Caving

Those who are looking for an experience with a bit more edge should sign up for one of the adventure tours that let you crawl and climb through caves lit only by your headlamp. The Plughole Tour, for example, starts with a 10m/yd abseil into the Elder Cave, and takes in roomy caverns and narrow tunnels before culminating in the Imperial Cave.

MOUNT TOMAH BOTANIC GARDEN

Take Jenolan Caves Road back to the Great Western Highway, and turn right towards Mount Victoria. From Mt Victoria, head north towards the township of Bell, from where you can make a detour to the **Zig Zag Railway** 9 *(see box, right)* by turning left or reach Mount Tomah by turning right. **Mount Tomah Botanic Garden** 10 (Bell's Line of Road; tel: 02 4567 2154;

www.rbgsyd.nsw.gov.au; Oct–Mar: daily 10am–5pm, Apr–Sept: 10am–4pm; charge) lies about 20 minutes down the road and is the cool-climate cousin of Sydney's Royal Botanic Gardens *(see p.39)*.

Highlights of the garden, spread over 11 hectares (28 acres), include the Rhododendron Collection and the Gondwana Forest Walk, which showcases the related plant species of the prehistoric super-continent of Gondwana that included Australia, New Zealand, South America and Africa. The walk includes a grove of extremely rare Wollemi pines (fewer than 100 are known to exist in the wild), the ancient species discovered in the Blue Mountains in 1994. The gardens have picnic facilities, including free electric barbecues, and a good restaurant.

From Mount Tomah, return to Sydney via Bells Line of Road to Richmond, from where signs will direct you back to the city.

Zig Zag Railway

Rail buffs will want to take a detour (signposted from Mount Victoria) to the Zig Zag Railway (tel: 02 6355 2955; www.zigzagrailway.com.au), a 13km (8-mile) full-size, narrow-gauge railway that descends the western escarpment of the mountains. It was built in the 1860s and operated until 1910, when a 10-tunnel deviation opened. Rail enthusiasts operate the line, with trains departing at 11am, 1pm and 3pm from Clarence station. The return journey takes around 90 minutes, and the engines are steam or diesel.

ROYAL NATIONAL PARK

The world's second-oldest national park covers 16,300 hectares (40,200 acres) of dense bushland, towering coastal cliffs, deep river valleys and pristine beaches, and lies just an hour south of Sydney.

Bush Camping
If you want to experience waking up in the bush, the Royal National Park has a number of camping sites. Call 02 9542 0683 (daily 10.30am–1.30pm) for more details.

DISTANCE 26km (16 miles)
TIME A full day
START/END Sydney
POINTS TO NOTE
This tour is best done by car. To access the park, head south from Sydney's CBD via the Princes Highway, following the signs to Sutherland and Wollongong. The route and the park entrance are well signposted. Remember to pack your swimsuit, sun cream and a picnic lunch; apart from kiosks stocking snacks, there are no food outlets in the park. The distance above is from Audley.

Of all the world's national parks, only Yellowstone in the US is older than Sydney's, which was created in 1879. Far from aiming to preserve the area's natural landscape, the park's founders tried to replicate London's Hampstead Heath, introducing manicured lawns and importing plants, rabbits, foxes and deer. Nowadays, the emphasis is firmly on protecting native flora and fauna, and the park has over 150km (90 miles) of walking trails for visitors to enjoy.

AUDLEY

The **Royal National Park Visitor Centre** (Sir Bertram Stevens Drive, Audley; tel: 02 9542 0648; daily 8.30am–4.30pm) lies 3km (2 miles) inside the park gates. This is a great place to pick up maps and information about the park. Facilities nearby include barbecues, picnic shelters, toilets and a small kiosk. The township of **Audley ❶** is a popular place with families, not least because it is possible to hire rowing boats, canoes and kayaks from the Audley Boatshed.

BUSH LANDSCAPE

From Audley, continue along Sir Bertram Stevens Drive for about 10 minutes, then take the turn off to Wattamolla. En route you will experience some of the park's dramatic bush landscapes, which include towering trees such as eucalypts, angophoras, turpentine and blackbutt trees.

The park is home to a wide range of fauna, including swamp wallabies, echidnas and marsupial mice. The animals you are most likely to come across, however, are some of the park's

200 species of bird, including honey-eaters and wattlebirds in the shrub-lands, and sea eagles and the occasional albatross at the coast.

WATTAMOLLA BEACH

Wattamolla Beach ❷ is one of the park's most popular beaches, thanks to its sheltered lagoon. There are picnic facilities here, and the trees that fringe the lagoon offer plenty of shade. From the car park you can also access a number of walks that form part of the park's 26km (16-mile) Coast Walk. The return walk from Wattamolla to Little Marley Beach, for instance, is a stunning clifftop walk that takes around two and half hours.

GARIE BEACH

Head back up Wattamolla Road to rejoin Sir Bertram Stevens Drive heading south. It will take about 15 minutes to reach the turn off for **Garie Beach ❸**, perhaps the park's prettiest beach. Surfers love the rolling breaks, but even if you are not into riding the waves, it is worth coming here just to admire the views that stretch up and down the coast.

FOREST PATH

Head back up Garie Road to rejoin Sir Bertram Stevens Drive heading south. After about 10 minutes, the entrance

to Lady Carrington Drive will be on your right. Park here and look for the entrance to the **Forest Path ❹**, just to the left of Lady Carrington Drive. This 90-minute looping bush walk passes through dense pockets of rain-forest. If you are very lucky, you may hear a whip bird (its call sounds like a stock whip being cracked) or spot such spectacular creatures as the lyre-bird, with its elaborate tail, or the irides-cent plumage of the satin bower bird.

Just past the Forest Path is McKell Avenue, a turn off to the settlement of Waterfall, which will lead you out of the park. From here, signs indicate the way back to Sydney.

Above from far left: peaceful beach in the Royal National Park; driving through an impressive avenue in the park; impressive coastal cliffs.

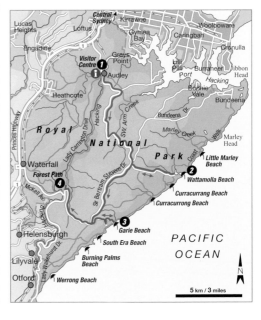

DIRECTORY

A user-friendly alphabetical listing of practical information, plus hand-picked hotels and restaurants, clearly organised by area, to suit all budgets and tastes. Select nightlife listings are also included here.

A

AGE RESTRICTIONS

It is legal to drink and purchase alcohol at 18 in Australia. The age of consent for heterosexual and homosexual relations in NSW is 16. Drivers may get their learner's licence at 16.

B

BUDGETING

Average costs (in Australian dollars) for a range of items are listed below:
- beer/glass of house wine: A$6
- main course at a budget restaurant: A$20
- main course at a moderate restaurant: A$30
- main course at an expensive restaurant: A$45
- cheap hotel: A$150
- moderate hotel: A$250
- deluxe hotel: A$350
- taxi to the airport: A$35
- single bus ticket: A$3.30
- TravelTen (10 bus rides): A$26.40
- My Multi Day Pass (can be used on bus, train and ferry): A$20

C

CHILDREN

Sydney is a great destination for families and children, with lots of parklands and beaches offering play opportunities, as well as exciting attractions. Children travel at reduced prices on public transport and pay reduced admission at most attractions. Most hotels offer babysitting services. At many hotels and child-friendly attractions, you will find a copy of *Sydney's Child*, a free monthly magazine with handy information and offers.

CLOTHING

Sydney is an informal and relaxed city with a temperate climate, which takes a lot of the stress out of packing. Concentrate on lightweight clothing that can be worn in layers if you are travelling in more temperate months. Even in winter, you will not need heavy woollies – a 12°C (54°F) day is considered by Sydneysiders to be very cold. Casual clothes are acceptable in most places, and barely anyone will bat an eyelid if you reveal some flesh. Just bear in mind that Sydneysiders are body-obsessed: those who have great bodies can and do show them off.

CONSULATES AND EMBASSIES

British Consulate General, Level 16, 1 Macquarie Place; tel: 02 9247 7521; www.ukinaustralia.fco.gov.uk.
Consulate General of Canada, Level 5, 111 Harrington Street; tel: 02 9364 3000; www.geo.international.gc.ca.

Consulate General of Ireland, Level 26, 1 Market Street; tel: 02 9264 9635; www.irishconsulatesydney.net.
Consulate General of the USA, MLC Centre, Level 59, 19–29 Martin Place; tel: 02 9373 9200; http://sydney.us consulate.gov.

CRIME AND SAFETY

Common-sense rules apply when visiting Sydney. As in any popular tourist destination, petty theft can be an issue at popular sights. Keep wallets out of sight, and don't leave valuables visible in the car or luggage unattended.

The inner city is, on the whole, quite safe. Despite its slightly unsavoury reputation, visitors to Kings Cross are unlikely to encounter trouble – unless they are looking for it – thanks to the constant urban buzz and a regular police presence. It is best to avoid Hyde Park after 10pm, though, particularly if you are on your own.

During off-peak periods, many city and suburban railway stations are either unstaffed or equipped with a skeleton staff. Look for 'night safe' areas on the platforms, which have security cameras and an intercom for contacting staff.

On a train, a blue light on one of the carriages indicates a guard is travelling in the carriage. Generally, public transport in the inner city is safe at any time of day. Avoid longer trips after 10pm, when there are fewer passengers.

CUSTOMS

Australia has extremely strict quarantine laws, to protect the agricultural industries and native Australian flora and fauna from introduced diseases. Animals, plants and their derivatives (feathers, untreated wood, fur, etc) must be declared on arrival, along with all foodstuffs, no matter how well packaged. All passengers must fill in an Incoming Passenger Card before disembarking the plane, which is checked by customs officers. There are serious penalties for false declarations. In many cases, you will be allowed to keep the items, as long as you declare them.

Anyone over the age of 18 is allowed to bring into Australia: A$900 worth of goods (A$450 for those under 18), not including alcohol or tobacco; 2.25l of alcohol (wine, beer or spirits); and 250 cigarettes or 250g of cigars and tobacco products other than cigarettes.

D

DISABLED TRAVELLERS

Sydney caters reasonably well for people with disabilities, but it is wise to start making enquiries and arrangements before leaving home. A good place to begin is the **National Information Communication Awareness Network (NICAN)**, a national organisation that keeps a database of facilities and services with disabled access,

Above from far left: kangaroos at the Koala Park and giraffe at Taronga Zoo – lots of animals, indigenous and otherwise, to appeal to children.

Australia Overseas
In the UK:
Australian High Commission, Australia House, The Strand, London WC2B 4LA; tel: 020-7379 4334; www.uk.embassy. gov.au.

In the US:
Australian Embassy, 1601 Massachusetts Avenue, NW Washington DC 20036; tel: 202-797 3000; www.usa. embassy.gov.au (plus consulates in New York, Los Angeles, San Francisco, Miami and Detroit).

In Canada:
Australian High Commission, Suite 710, 50 O'Connor Street, Ottawa, ON K1P 6L2; tel: 613-236 0841; www. ahc-ottawa.org.

including accommodation and tourist sights. It also keeps track of the range of publications on the subject.

IDEAS (Information on Disability Awareness and Education Services) also offers online databases on disability services, equipment suppliers and accessible travel, plus other speciality information from other agencies.

Most larger hotels – apart from the more moderately priced ones – have lifts. Metro Monorail and LightRail services are wheelchair-accessible, as are some buses (indicated on timetables available at bus stops or online at www.sydneybuses.info).

NICAN, tel: 1800 806 769; www.nican.com.au.

IDEAS, tel: 1800 029 904; www.ideas.org.au.

E

ELECTRICITY

The Australian power supply is 220–240 volts AC. Sockets are three flat-pin plugs and electrical items from the US and Europe, including the UK, will require an adaptor plug.

EMERGENCIES

Police, Fire, Ambulance: tel: 000.
Hotel Doctor Service: tel: 02 9962 6000.
Dental Emergency Information Service: tel: 02 9369 7050.

ETIQUETTE

Australians take a casual approach to matters of etiquette: it is unusual to greet the assistant when you walk into shop, for instance. If you are greeting someone, saying 'G'day' will instantly mark you out as a tourist; 'Hello' and 'Hi' are much more commonly used. Australians are far less likely than Europeans to open doors for women, although it is not unheard of. The one rule of etiquette no Australian will break: if someone 'shouts' you (buys you a drink), the next round is your turn. Similarly, it is considered bad form not to bring along some kind of alcoholic beverage if you are invited to someone's house for dinner.

F

FESTIVALS

Sydney's favourite festivals are grand spectaculars, whether they involve the drag and dazzle of the Gay and Lesbian Mardi Gras or the spectacular harbour firework celebrations on New Year's Eve. These are some of the city's best:

January
Sydney Festival: Three weeks of local and international arts.
Australia Day (26 Jan): Various harbour-centred events, including the inevitable fireworks.

February

Chinese New Year: Lion dances, parades, markets and other festivities centred around Chinatown.

February/March

Gay and Lesbian Mardi Gras: a parade, party and associated arts festival.

Easter

Royal Easter Show: The country comes to town; from wood-chopping to cattle contests.

May

Sydney Writers Festival: A varied programme of readings, public lectures and panel events, many of which are free.

June

Sydney Film Festival: Two weeks of local and international cinema, centred around the gorgeous State Theatre.

September

Spring Racing Carnival: Sydney's premier horse racing event is the place to be seen.

December

Sydney to Hobart Yacht Race: Thousands flock to the foreshore to watch the start of the race.

New Year's Eve

The biggest party of them all; if you want to nab a foreshore position for the fireworks, be prepared to camp out all day.

FURTHER READING

Aboriginal Australia

Archaeology of the Dreaming, Josephine Flood.

Dreamings: The Art of Aboriginal Australia, edited by Peter Sutton.
The Whispering in Our Hearts, Henry Reynolds.

Art and Architecture

The Art of Australia, Robert Hughes.
Sydney: A Guide to Recent Architecture, Francesca Morrison.
Sydney Architecture, Graham Jahn.

Biography

A Fence Around the Cuckoo, Ruth Park.
30 Days in Sydney, Peter Carey.
Unreliable Memoirs, Clive James.

Fiction

For Love Alone, Christina Stead.
A Harp in the South, Ruth Park.
Oscar and Lucinda, Peter Carey.
Poor Man's Orange, Ruth Park.
The Service of Clouds, Delia Falconer.

Food and Wine

The Penguin Good Australian Wine Guide, Mark Shield and Huon Hooke.
The SBS Eating Guide, Maeve O'Mara and Joanna Savill.
The Sydney Morning Herald Good Food Guide, edited by Terry Durack and Jill Dupleix.
The Wines of Australia, Oliver Mayo.

History

The Fatal Shore, Robert Hughes.
The Future Eaters, Tim Flannery.

Above: the Sydney skyline by night.

Festival Lowdown
For further information on festivals and events in Sydney check www.sydney festivals.com.au and www.cityof sydney.nsw.gov.au.

Leviathan, John Birmingham.
A Secret Country, John Pilger.

Travel Companions
Best Sydney Bushwalks, Neil Paton.
A Companion Guide to Sydney, Ruth Park.
Cosmopolitan Sydney: Explore the World in One City, Jock Collins and Antonio Castillo.
Sydney, Jan Morris.
The Sydney Morning Herald Best of Sydney, edited by Ross Muller.

G

GAY AND LESBIAN ISSUES

Sydney is one of the world's queer capitals, where homosexuality is not only legal (the age of consent is 16), but homosexuals are legally protected against discrimination and defamation. That does not mean there is no homophobia, of course, but the inner city – particularly the gay hotspots of Darlinghurst and Newtown – is particularly gay-friendly, as you will see most spectacularly during the annual gay Mardi Gras.

Held each February, Mardi Gras is a three-week-long party, ending in a parade and huge ticket-only all-night dance party. Useful resources before your visit include sites such as www.pridecentre.com.au, www.pinkboard.com.au and www.dreadedned.

com.au, where you will find information on bars, clubs, restaurants, hotels, saunas and shops. Once you arrive, pick up a copy of the two free weekly gay mags, *Sydney Star Observer* and *Q Magazine*, for up-to-date information.

GREEN ISSUES

Australia has the unhappy distinction of having one of the most fragile environments on earth, as well as one of the world's largest per capita ecological footprints, which makes climate change a major issue for the country. After years of neglect by the Coalition government of Prime Minster John Howard, environmental issues are being addressed by the Labor government that has been in power since 2007, although major issues such as carbon limits and tackling the country's salinity crisis are proving to have no easy solutions.

On a day-to-day level, however, Australians are quite environmentally aware, dutifully recycling paper, plastics and glass, and being very anti-littering. The city's biggest environmental events are both held in March. Clean Up Australia Day sounds exactly like what it is, while Earth Hour, a now-global initiative that launched in Sydney in 2007, turns the city's lights off for an hour to demonstrate a commitment to combating climate change.

H

HEALTH

Healthcare and Insurance

The UK and Ireland have reciprocal healthcare agreements with Australia that entitle visitors to free hospital treatment through the Medicare system. This does not cover all eventualities, however; ambulance and dental treatment, for instance, are not included. All travellers should take out their own travel insurance, and check the fine print to see whether you need to register with Medicare before making a claim.

Inoculations

No vaccinations are required for entry to Australia, unless you have been in an epidemic zone or a yellow fever-, cholera- or typhoid-infested area in the six days prior to your arrival.

Pharmacies and Hospitals

Chemists (pharmacies) are a great place to get advice on minor ailments such as bites, scratches and stomach trouble. They will also tell you where the nearest medical centre is. If you have a prescription from your doctor that you want to get filled in Australia, you will need to have it endorsed by a local medical practitioner. While most public hospitals have emergency departments, these are notoriously overstretched. For anything that is not a major condition, you are advised to find the nearest medical centre instead. The **Crest Hotel Pharmacy** (91–93 Darlinghurst Road; tel: 02 9358 1822) in Kings Cross is open from 8am to midnight, seven days a week.

HOURS AND HOLIDAYS

Business hours are generally 9am to 5pm Monday to Friday. Shops will generally stay open to 6pm on weekdays and 9pm on Thursdays, with weekend opening hours usually 10am to 5pm on Saturdays and 10am to 4pm on Sundays. Banks, post offices and most shops close on the following public holidays:

1 Jan New Year's Day.
26 Jan Australia Day.
Mar/Apr Good Friday, Easter Monday.
25 Apr Anzac Day.
June (2nd Mon) Queen's Birthday.
Aug (1st Mon) Bank Holiday.
Oct (1st Mon) Labour Day.
25 Dec Christmas Day.
26 Dec Boxing Day.

I

INTERNET FACILITIES

Some Sydney cafes offer Wi-Fi access to patrons (usually for the price of a cup of coffee), but Internet cafes tend to be the more popular option. They are particularly common in the backpacker hub of Kings Cross. Try **Global Gossip** (63 Darlinghurst Road, Kings Cross;

Above from far left: out and proud; sunbathers at Bondi Beach taking advantage of the sunny climate.

Anzac Day
Possibly Australia's most important national holiday, Anzac Day commemorates the first major military action fought by Australian and New Zealand forces during World War I when they landed at Gallipoli on 25 April 1915. Over 8,000 Australian soldiers died in the eight-month long Allied offensive.

www.globalgossip.com), with branches around the city, or **Central Internet Cafe** (1/230 Elizabeth Street, Surry Hills; www.centralinternetcafe.com.au).

L

LEFT LUGGAGE

Sydney's stations do not provide left-luggage facilities.

LOST PROPERTY

There are separate lost-property offices at each Sydney bus depot. To contact the appropriate depot, visit www.sydney buses.info/lost-property.htm.

CityRail's lost-property office is located at Central Station, opposite platform 1, and is open from 8.30am to 4.20pm Monday to Friday. Call 02 9379 3341, or fill in an online request at www.cityrailinfo/contact-us/lost-property if you need to report a loss.

M

MAPS

You can pick up regional maps at the Sydney Visitor Centre (corner of Argyle and Playfair streets, The Rocks; tel: 02 9255 1788; www.shfa.nsw.gov.au; daily 9.30am–5.30pm). You can download bus maps from www.sydneybuses.info; newsagents usually also carry maps for local bus routes.

MEDIA

Print Media

Sydney has just one broadsheet newspaper, *The Sydney Morning Herald*, and one tabloid, *The Daily Telegraph*. The national broadsheet, *The Australian*, and the national business newspaper, *The Australian Financial Review*, are also widely available. A weekly entertainment guide comes free with Friday's *Herald*, and many free visitor-oriented publications are available at hotels and other tourist destinations. The monthly *Time Out* and free street press such as *Drum Media* available in pubs and record shops, etc are useful.

Radio

Sydney has a broad range of radio stations to choose from, with popular FM stations including ABC Classic FM (92.9) for classical; MIX 106.5FM for music that falls between rock and pop; and the ABC's youth station, Triple J (105.9), for alternative music.

Television

Australia's five free-to-air channels have been instrumental in rolling out digital television, with 15 digital stations now available, and more to come. The national broadcaster, the ABC, has the best national news and current affairs coverage; the other government-run station, the more internationally oriented SBS, features dramas, documentaries and movies from around the

world, as well as international news. The commercial channels, Seven, Nine and Ten, are fairly interchangeable, although Ten caters to a younger audience than the other two. Satellite television is available in most hotels.

MONEY

Cash Machines

There are hundreds of Automatic Teller Machines (ATMs) around the city, allowing for easy withdrawal of cash.

Credit Cards

American Express, Visa and Master-Card are all readily accepted, with Diners Club less popular. Some restaurants and companies levy a credit-card charge, usually around 1 or 2 percent.

Currency

The local currency is the Australian dollar (abbreviated as A$ or simply $), made up of 100 cents. Coins come in 5-, 10-, 20- and 50-cent units, and A$1 and A$2 units. Notes come in A$5, A$10, A$20, A$50 and A$100 denominations. Where prices feature single cents, these are rounded up or down to the nearest 5 cents.

Taxes

A Goods and Services Tax (GST) of 10 percent is levied virtually across the board (there are a few exemptions). By law, the GST must be included in the advertised price of an item.

Tipping

Australians are generally fairly relaxed about tipping. While it has become common to leave 10 percent at a restaurant, it is not customary to tip taxi drivers, hairdressers, bar staff or porters at airports.

Travellers' Cheques

All well-known Australian-dollar travellers' cheques can be cashed at airports, banks, hotels and similar establishments. Banks offer the best exchange rates on cheques in foreign currencies; most banks charge a fee for cashing cheques.

P

POLICE

In an emergency, dial 000; for non-emergency enquiries, telephone police assistance on 131 444.

POST

The government-run Australia Post delivers an efficient service. Buy your stamps and post your letters at any post office (expect to pay A$1.45 to send a postcard to Europe or the US, and A$2.20 for a standard letter). There are plenty of red post boxes on the streets that you can also use. Yellow post boxes are for the Overnight Express service, which delivers to most places in Australia and costs extra. (To use this service, you need to buy a special enve-

Above from far left: street entertainer on George Street; the city's enticing blend of old and new architecture.

Sydney Bookshops
Good bookstores in Sydney include:
• Dymocks (424 George Street; www.dymocks.com.au);
• Kinokunyia (500 George Street; www.kinokuniya.com);
• Borders Bondi Junction (500 Oxford Street; www.borders.com.au).

lope at the post office.) The General Post Office (GPO) is located in Martin Place, on the corner of George Street, www.austpost.com.au.

R

RELIGION

The Australian Constitution specifically prohibits the establishment of a state religion, but according to the latest census, around two-thirds of Australians still identify themselves as Christians. The next most popular religions are Buddhism and Islam. As in many other Western countries, the integration of Islamic communities has become an issue which flares up periodically. On the whole, however, Australia remains a tolerant, diverse nation.

S

SMOKING

Australia has strong anti-smoking legislation that bans smoking inside offices, shopping centres, restaurants, public buildings, licensed premises, public transport and even on some beaches.

T

TELEPHONES

To call Sydney from outside the country, dial your international access code followed by 61 for Australia and 2 for Sydney. To call anywhere else in Australia from Sydney, dial the area code (eg 03 for Melbourne, 07 for Brisbane), followed by the number. You do not need to dial 02 to call a Sydney number when in Sydney, nor do you add 02 to six-digit numbers beginning with 13.

To call internationally from Sydney, dial 0011 followed by the relevant country code (Canada 1, Ireland 353, UK 44, US 1).

Public phone boxes are hard to find and their design means they are noisy to use if you do; your best bet is a station or major post office.

Mobile (Cell) Phones

Australia uses the 900MHz and 1,800MHz GSM bands for mobile phones. Many North American phones, which are CDMA-band only, will not work in Australia. If you want to buy a local SIM card, you can purchase one at the many mobile-phone shops throughout the city. Expect to pay around A$20–30. A phone and SIM card pack, with a basic phone and around A$10 in phone credit, can start as low as around A$60.

Before buying a phone or SIM card, check which areas are covered, as different service providers offer different levels of coverage (although all will work in the main cities). Note that in Australia, the person calling the mobile phone pays; receiving a call on a mobile is free.

TIME ZONES

Sydney is on Eastern Standard Time (along with the rest of New South Wales, Queensland, Victoria and Tasmania). This is GMT +10. At noon in Sydney, it is 2am in London, and 9pm the day before in New York.

During the summer, New South Wales observes Daylight Saving Time, moving the clock forward by one hour between the first Sunday in October and the last Sunday in March. At noon in Sydney, it is therefore 1am in London, and 8pm the day before in New York.

TOILETS

Pay-to-use public toilets are fairly common on Sydney streets, but you can generally use the facilities at any pub or department store free of charge without making a purchase. Toilets are generally well maintained.

TOURIST INFORMATION

The Sydney Visitor Centre (corner of Argyle and Playfair streets, The Rocks; tel: 02 9255 1788; www.shfa.nsw.gov.au; daily 9.30am–5.30pm) is a useful resource for travellers, with plenty of printed material and knowledgeable staff. The website also has some helpful features to access before your trip, including the ability to book accommodation for you.

TOURS AND GUIDES

A harbour cruise remains a must-do for many visitors, although you can get a very similar experience at a much cheaper price simply by catching a ferry to a destination such as Taronga Zoo or Manly. A number of operators offer a wide range of similar cruises: among the most experienced is Captain Cook Cruises (www.captaincook.com.au/sydney). Other options include include sailing on an authentic timber tall ship, courtesy of Sydney Tall Ships (www.sydneytallships.com.au), or the unique Tribal Warrior cruise, which offers an indigenous perspective (www.tribalwarrior.org).

TRANSPORT

Arrival

By Air

Many international airlines land at Sydney's international airport, Kingsford Smith Airport at Mascot, approximately 8km (5 miles) from the city centre. AirportLink trains (www.airportlink.com.au) run to and from Central Station up to eight times an hour on weekdays, and four times an hour at weekends; the journey takes 12 minutes, and a single adult journey costs around A$15.

Many hotels run shuttle buses to the airport. A taxi to the city centre will cost about A$30 and take about 20 minutes in light traffic. Each terminal has its own taxi rank.

Above from far left: see the city from above for stunning views; boats of all sizes in Sydney harbour.

Carbon-Offsetting Air travel produces a huge amount of carbon dioxide and is a major contributor to global warming. If you would like to offset the damage caused to the environment by your flight, a number of organisations can do this for you, using online 'carbon calculators', which tell you how much you need to donate. In the UK travellers can visit www.climatecare.org or www.carbonneutral.com; in the US log on to www.climatefriendly.com or www.sustainabletravelinternational.org.

Tickets and Passes

Most locals use a TravelTen bus ticket (colour-coded depending on which areas you want to travel in). These are good because a number of buses are prepay only, so you need already to have purchased your ticket; they also offer (small) savings. There are combined monorail/light rail one- and three-day passes, but these do not work with any other form of transport. If you are staying for a week and travelling every day, consider using a MyMulti, which can be used on buses, trains and ferries. This can be good value if you are going to be doing a lot of travelling. You can also get a MyMulti DayPass, a one-day ticket for bus, train and ferry, but you would need to be covering a huge amount of territory to make this worthwhile.

If you intend to hire a car, all the major companies have offices at the airport terminals.

By Sea

If time and money permit, there is no better introduction to this harbour city than arriving by boat. Ocean liners berth at the Overseas Passenger Terminal in Circular Quay and at Barangaroo.

Getting Around

Buses

Sydney's extensive bus service has its main termini at Circular Quay, Wynyard and Central Station. Red Sydney Explorer and blue Bondi Explorer hop-on hop-off buses leave regularly from Circular Quay and run in a continuous loop around the city's main attractions. You can buy a one- or a two-day (valid for any two days out of eight) ticket. For timetables or routes see Transport Infoline; tel: 131 500; www.131500.com.au. A free CBD shuttle (route no. 555) operates every 10 minutes during peak hours (Mon–Fri 9.30am–3.30pm, Sat–Sun 9.30am–6pm).

Driving

Sydneysiders have a reputation for being aggressive drivers, which many blame on the hazards facing the city's motorists: congestion, frequent toll roads, the difficulty of finding parking anywhere in the city – and, if you do find it, the cost of parking meters – and speed limits that can change several times in the space of a few kilometres. However, drivers follow the road rules; so as long as you are comfortable driving on the left, you will be fine.

One thing to beware of is drink-driving. There are heavy penalties for this; up to imprisonment for serious transgression. Random breath-testing is common. The limit for licensed drivers is 0.05g per 100ml.

Hiring a car in Australia is expensive by international standards. The main companies – Avis, Hertz and Budget – have near-identical prices. Small outfits may offer cheaper rates, but may not provide the same coverage as the major companies. Overseas drivers aged 18 or older only need to be in possession of an up-to-date driving licence from their home country. For information about road rules visit www.rta.nsw.gov.au/rules regulations/roadrules.

Ferries

Sydney's most picturesque form of transport is loved by both commuters and tourists; most services begin and end at Circular Quay. Tickets and timetables can be found at the ferries office here, or at www.sydneyferries.info.

Metro Light Rail and Monorail

The Light Rail links the CBD with the inner-west suburbs, while the monorail is an elevated track around Darling Harbour, Chinatown and the CBD. For more information on either service, visit www.metrotransport.com.au.

Taxis

Taxis can be hailed in the street or at a taxi rank, and should run on a meter. There is an initial A$3.20 charge, then A$1.93 per km thereafter. This rises by 20 percent between 10pm and 6am. Booking a taxi by phone will incur surcharges, as will journeys on toll roads. Companies include:

Premier Cabs, tel: 131 017.
Taxis Combined, tel: 133 300.
Legion Cabs, tel: 131 451.
For more information, visit www.nsw taxi.org.au.

Water taxis are a handy way for getting to waterfront attractions, but can be expensive unless several of you share the cost. Water Taxis Combined, tel: 02 9555 888; www.watertaxis.com.au.

Trains

Cityrail services provide fast links through Sydney's inner city and the suburbs, but tend to be very congested at peak hours. Trains run until midnight, when they are replaced by a Nightrider bus service. All suburban lines stop at Town Hall and Central Station, which is also Sydney's main terminal for regional and interstate trains.

V

VISAS AND PASSPORTS

Visitors to Australia must have a passport valid for the entire period of their stay. Anyone who is not an Australian citizen also needs a visa, which must be obtained before leaving home, except for New Zealand citizens, who are issued with a visa on arrival in Australia.

Most visitors can obtain a visa online, using either the eVisitor service for European visitors (www.immi.gov.au/e_visa/evisitor.htm) or the Electronic Transfer Authority (www.eta.immi.gov.au) for visitors from other countries including the USA. Visas are generally valid for 12 months, with no stay exceeding three months. An online fee of around A$20 applies. Tourist visas for longer than three months must be obtained from an embassy or consulate. Extending a visa depends on the visa type. ETAs and eVisitors cannot be extended; if you wanted to stay, you would need to apply for a different type of visa at least two weeks before your other visa expired.

W

WEBSITES

Useful websites for sights and attractions are listed throughout the book. Try also www.sydneyguide.net.au, www.sydney.com.au, www.sydneyaustralia.com and www.eatability.com.au.

WEIGHTS AND MEASURES

Australia uses the metric system of weights, measures and temperatures.

Above: taxi by night.

Women

At time of writing, the Lord Mayor of Sydney, the Governor of NSW, the Governor-General and the Prime Minister were all women, suggesting that women in Australia enjoy a reasonable amount of equality. True, women typically still earn less than men – as they do almost everywhere in the world – but Australia was the second country in the world to give women the vote, and has on the whole protected their interests relatively well.

Perhaps surprisingly, you do not have to spend a fortune to sleep well in Sydney. Yes, at the city's most famous hotels, the ones where every window frames its own harbour view, prices can soar up towards the stratosphere. But in the CBD and districts such as Darling Harbour, there are lots of mid- and budget-priced options. Neighbourhoods such as Potts Point and Darlinghurst are home to some hidden gems that combine central locations with loads of charm and style.

CBD

Amora Hotel Jamison Street

11 Jamison Street; tel: 02 9696 2500; www.amorajamisonhotel sydney.com; train: Wynyard; $$$

While the big names battle it out amongst themselves, the Amora has kept a lower profile, offering its discerning guests a stylish inner-city experience at great rates. All the rooms have marble bathrooms and mod cons including Internet access and computer game consoles, but ask for one with harbour or city view. The hotel's secret weapon is its divine Angsana Day Spa, the perfect place for a bit of pampering.

Price for a double room for one night without breakfast:

$$$$	over A$350
$$$	A$250–350
$$	A$150–250
$	below A$150

Australian Heritage Hotel

100 Cumberland Street, The Rocks; tel: 02 9247 2229; www.australian heritagehotel.com; $

If you like your accommodation served up with a slice of history, this bed and breakfast is the place for you. Housed in a typical Federation-style pub in The Rocks, the location means it is easy to stroll down to the harbour, into the heart of the city or around Sydney's oldest district. Rooms are tastefully decorated with antiques, and the roof terrace is the perfect place to soak up a harbour view along with a cold beer at the end of the day. One word of warning: bathroom facilities are shared.

Base Sydney

477 Kent Street; tel: 02 9267 7718; www.stayatbase.com; train: Town Hall; $

Youth hostels are not what they used to be, and nowhere proves the point better than Base. Accommodation ranges from twin rooms to multi-bed dormitories, all of which feature surprisingly stylish furnishings. There are added extras, such as free use of the solarium, personal underbed storage lockers and a women-only floor, The Sanctuary.

Establishment

5 Bridge Lane; tel: 02 9240 3100; www.merivale.com.au; train: Wynyard; $$$–$$$$

It would be possible – if expensive – to spend an entire week in Sydney, drinking only at venues owned by the Hemmes family, purveyors of super-slick bars and clubs including those contained in Establishment and The Ivy Bar *(see p.122)*. They also offer accommodation at Establishment: 31 super-chic rooms and two penthouse suites. The decor varies across the rooms, but if you think black timber floorboards and lilac suede daybeds, along with Bulgari toiletries, you are heading in the right direction.

Four Seasons

199 George Street, The Rocks; tel: 02 9250 3100; www.fourseasons. com; $$$–$$$$

Much of Sydney life revolves around attaining a harbour view; check in to the Four Seasons, and that is one thing you will not have to worry about. In addition to sweeping vistas across the harbour taking in the Opera House and the Botanic Gardens, the Four Seasons offers large rooms tastefully done in neutral tones; an outdoor pool; and that famous Four Seasons attention to detail.

Fraser Suites

488 Kent Street; tel: 02 8823 8888; www.fraserhospitality.com; train: Town Hall; $$$

'Sexy' is not usually a word applied to serviced apartments, but then, most serviced apartments do not feature a

6m (20ft) rainfall chandelier in the lobby. This all-studio complex, designed by internationally renowned architects Foster & Partners, is both sexy and luxurious. There is fine bone china in the kitchens, a huge gym and – bliss – windows that actually open. A wonderful treat.

Hilton Hotel

488 George Street; tel: 02 9266 2000; www.hiltonsydney.com.au; $$$

If your choice of a hotel hinges upon on how cool its bar or restaurant is, the Hilton is for you. Zeta Bar is a chic spot to savour a drink or two, while the hotel's premier restaurant, Glass Brasserie, is overseen by one of Australia's top chefs, Luke Mangan. Add a central location and sleek, spacious guest rooms, and it is no wonder the Hilton is popular.

The Observatory Hotel

89–113 Kent Street, The Rocks; tel: 02 9256 2222; www.observatory hotel.com.au; $$$$

The Observatory Hotel offers old-school luxury: Edwardian furnishings and a personal approach that is not easy to sustain in a hotel with 96 rooms. Repeat guests love the hotel's traditional afternoon teas; the clubby feel of the bar; and the spa, where you can do backstroke in a 20m (65ft) pool gazing at the ceiling with its twinkling map of the southern hemisphere's constellations.

Above from far left: bathroom at the Amora Hotel Jamison Street; expect space and stylish decor at the Hilton.

Park Hyatt Hotel

7 Hickson Road, The Rocks; tel: 02 9241 1234; www.sydney.park. hyatt.com; $$$$

They say there are three rules in real estate – location, location, location – and locations do not get better than this. The low-rise sandstone hotel hugs the foreshore smack bang opposite the Opera House. If you really need more convincing, the super-spacious rooms come with butler service and sink-into marble tubs. Guests can also treat themselves to swim in the rooftop pools, or a meal in the acclaimed dining room.

Shangri-La Hotel

176 Cumberland Street, The Rocks; tel: 02 9250 6000; www.shangrila. com; $$$

One of a handful of serious contenders for the title of Sydney's Best Hotel, the Shangri-La still manages to deliver personalised service despite its 500-plus rooms. And it gets better from there. The guest rooms, each of which has a harbour view, are supersized: the smallest are 40 sq m (430 sq ft). Guests also enjoy complimen-

tary broadband access, and one of the city's most stunning cocktail bars, Blu Bar *(see p.122)*.

Darling Harbour and Around

Novotel Rockford Darling Harbour

17 Little Pier Street, Darling Harbour; tel: 02 8217 4000; www.accor hotels.com; $$$

Another favourite hotel for families. The rooms themselves are bright, spacious and airy, and the pool is a great way for kids to burn off excess energy. The location is also close to key family attractions such as Sydney Aquarium and the Powerhouse Museum.

Oaks Goldsbrough Apartments

243 Pyrmont Street, Darling Harbour; tel: 02 8586 2500; www.theoaksgroup.com.au; $–$$

The Goldsbrough Apartments offer the best of both worlds: sleek, modern interiors set in a historic building dating back to 1883. The lovely neoclassical facade hides a property where airy dimensions, local hardwood floors and exposed columns add a romantic ambience to the selection of studios, one- and two-bedroom apartments. Fitness fans are catered for with a lap pool, spa, sauna and gymnasium.

Quest on Dixon

8 Dixon Street, Darling Harbour;

Price for a double room for one night without breakfast:

$$$$	over A$350
$$$	A$250–350
$$	A$150–250
$	below A$150

tel: 02 8281 4700; www.queston dixon.com.au; $–$$

Comfortable, furnished apartments in both studio and one-bedroom layouts – some with private balconies – make Quest on Dixon another popular choice with families. Travelling gourmets may also like to consider this hotel for its proximity to a wide array of won't-break-the-bank dining options. Darling Harbour, Cockle Bay and Liverpool Street's Spanish quarter are all nearby, but best of all are the many mouth-watering eateries of Chinatown. The hotel also has 'charge back' arrangements with several local restaurants, that let you order in dinner, with the price of your meal simply added to your bill.

Vulcan Hotel

500 Wattle Street, Ultimo; tel: 02 9211 3283; www.vulcan hotel.com.au; $–$$

The stylish Vulcan Hotel is one of Sydney's hidden gems – quite an achievement for a hotel that first started welcoming guests back in 1894. Located in a National Heritage-listed building close to Darling Harbour, this boutique hotel's 46 rooms include doubles, triples and studios in a variety of configurations. The interiors, including the private landscaped courtyard, offer oodles of urban chic, and the service is both intimate and friendly. Highly recommended.

Bayview Boulevard Sydney

90 William Street, Woolloomooloo; tel: 1800 671 222; www.bayview hotels.com; $$

This old Sydney stalwart was fully renovated a few years ago, and now offers many of the benefits of the best hotels in town, without the price tag. Many of the rooms have stunning harbour and city views, and feature mod cons such as Internet access. The location is also terrific, just 15 minutes' walk from the heart of town and the hip spots of Darlinghurst. Great for both business and leisure travellers.

Blue Sydney

6 Cowper Wharf Road, Woolloomooloo; tel: 02.9331 9000; www.tajhotels.com; $$$

There is a lot to love about this hotel located in one of Sydney's historic timber wharves. The rooms are stylish; the hotel's bars are buzzing; some of Sydney's best restaurants are on your doorstep. Then there's the waterside location, and the celebrated Taj Hotels service. Some of the rooms are on the small side, but who spends a lot of time in their room in Sydney?

Hotel 59

59 Bayswater Road, Rushcutters Bay; tel: 02 9360 5900; www.hotel59.com.au; $

Located in a quiet section of Bayswater Road, this small hotel offers just

Above from far left: a hotel room at the Shangri-La with unbeatable views of Sydney's harbour; exterior of the Vulcan Hotel.

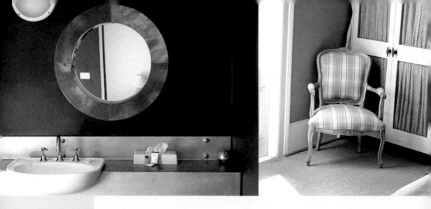

nine cheerful, spotlessly clean, no-frills rooms and self-catering family accommodation. Excellent cooked breakfasts are included in the price.

Vibe Hotel

100 Bayswater Road,
Rushcutters Bay; tel: 8353 8988;
www.vibehotels.com.au; $$

There are a number of Vibe Hotels in Sydney, but location-wise, this is the pick of the bunch. The bayside setting is close to the hip neighbourhoods of Darlinghurst and Potts Point, and not far from the city centre. Vibe takes a fresh, friendly approach, updating standard hotel rooms with a funky flair while still offering all the amenities and services that you would expect.

Darlinghurst and Surry Hills

The Chelsea

49 Womerah Avenue, Darlinghurst;
tel: 02 9380 5994; email: xchelsea@
ozemail.com.au; $–$$

Many Sydneysiders spend some time living in Womerah Avenue, drawn by its sprawling terraces (great shared accommodation material) and its proximity to the inner city's most pumping venues. Those selling points are at the heart of The Chelsea, a 13-room boutique hotel tucked into two 1870s terrace houses. Elegant interiors and a serene courtyard have a European feel. The double rooms have en-suite bathrooms, while the four singles have shared facilities.

Hotel Altamont

207 Darlinghurst Road, Darlinghurst;
tel: 02 9360 6000; www.altamont.
com.au; train: Kings Cross; $$

The building that houses the Altamont is rich in history of all kinds. The colonial building was modelled on Sydney's original Government House; many years later, it housed the Cauldron nightclub, an infamous haunt for music-industry types and other party animals. These days it is home to a boutique hotel that is one of the best budget offerings in town. The decor proves that 'budget' doesn't have to mean cheap or cookie-cutter; the location is right in the heart of Darlinghurst; and in true rock-star fashion, late check-outs are encouraged.

Medusa

267 Darlinghurst Rd, Darlinghurst;
tel: 02 9331 1000;
www.medusa.com.au; $$$

If your plans for your Sydney visit includes plenty late-night clubbing and lots of shopping, Medusa is where you will want to stay. It boasts a central loca-

Price for a double room for one night without breakfast:	
$$$$	over A$350
$$$	A$250–350
$$	A$150–250
$	below A$150

tion on funky Darlinghurst Road; a decor that is heavy on big, bold colours; plushly upholstered furniture; and free gym membership for every guest. This all draws a chic crowd that, according to rumour, includes Kylie Minogue. With just 18 rooms, the Medusa offers an intimate welcome that also extends to guests who bring their dogs with them.

Paddington and Woollahra

The Hughenden

14 Queen Street, Woollahra; tel: 02 9363 4863; www.hughenden hotel.com.au; $$–$$$

Plenty of Sydneysiders fantasise about living in one of the grand mansions lining Woollahra's leafy streets: a stay at The Hughenden lets you try the fantasy on for size. Housed in an Italianite mansion dating back to 1876, the hotel is run by a pair of creative sisters (one a painter, one a writer), who create a welcoming atmosphere that includes afternoon tea in the lobby.

Bondi

Ravesis

Campbell Parade, Bondi Beach; tel: 02 9365 4422; www.ravesis.com.au; $$$

Now this is the way to do Bondi. A prime beachside location. An intimate atmosphere, with just 12 sleek, light-filled rooms. Your own balcony, complimentary Wi-Fi, and an in-house bar and restaurant. And in less than five minutes, you can be plunging into the surf. Perfect.

Blue Mountains

Broomelea Bed and Breakfast

273 Leura Mall, Leura; tel: 02 4784 2940; www.broomelea.com.au; $$

This gorgeous Federation bed and breakfast is nestled in leafy surrounds just a short stroll away from Leura's shops. The cosy rooms have four-poster beds and fireplaces, and the guest lounge is a lovely place to relax after dinner.

Echoes

3 Lilianfels Avenue, Katoomba; tel: 02 4782 1966; www.echoeshotel.com.au; $$$$

With just 12 rooms, two suites – all individually designed – and a private spa and sauna, this boutique hotel is like having your own amazing holiday house that comes complete with jaw-dropping views of the Jamison Valley. A pre-dinner drink in the glamorous bar or on the terrace is an absolute must.

Lilianfels

Lilianfels Blue Mountains Resort & Spa, Echo Point, Katoomba; tel: 02 4780 1200; www.lilianfels.com.au; $$$$

The ultimate Blue Mountains retreat, set in a historic country house amid 1 hectare (2½ acres) of manicured gardens. Lilianfels has an indulgent spa, a superb fine-dining restaurant, and is just 10 minutes' walk from the Three Sisters. Bliss.

Above from far left: chic bathroom at the Hotel Altamont; elegant interiors at The Chelsea; a tranquil deluxe courtyard room at the Hotel Altamont.

Whether you are in the mood for world-class fine dining, super-fresh seafood by the ocean or a cheap and cheerful feast, you will find myriad options in Sydney. The city's chefs have adapted to a wide range of cuisines, so you are as likely to find Asian flavours served up in a five-star dining room as in a hole-in-the-wall diner.

Sydneysiders have a reputation for being fickle diners, and it is true that the list of hottest dining spots in town changes with tedious regularity. However, there is enough loyalty to ensure the best restaurants in town remain busy most nights of the week. If you are planning a meal in a top restaurant, or one anywhere near the water, it is always advisable to book ahead.

No single suburb of Sydney can claim to be the main dining precinct in the city; eateries are scattered throughout the inner city, although it is a fairly good bet that if you find a nice bit of waterfront, there will be a couple of quality restaurants nearby. Darlinghurst and Surry Hills in particular offer an impressive array of dining options to suit every budget.

> Price for a two-course meal for one person with a glass of house wine:
>
> | | |
> |------|----------|
> | $$$$ | over A$90 |
> | $$$ | A$70–90 |
> | $$ | A$50–70 |
> | $ | below A$50 |

CBD

Din Tai Fung

World Square Shopping Centre, 644 George Street; tel: 02 9264 6010; www.dintaifung.com.tw; daily L, D; $

Dumpling heaven. This Taiwanese chain has outlets all over the world, and all over the world you will find diners queuing out the door day and night. The Sydney outlet is no exception. The massive menu offers a bewildering array of dumplings, but ignore the soup dumplings – thin-skinned, juicy morsels filled with pork and broth – at your peril. A total taste sensation.

est.

252 George Street; tel: 02 9240 3010; www.merivale.com.au; Mon–Fri L, D, Sat D; $$$$

Est. represents a meeting of the minds of two compelling Sydney characters. On the one hand, the king of wining and dining, owner Justin Hemmes provides the elegant dining room in his Establishment complex; on the other, Peter Doyle, who delivers the superb Modern Australian food such as steamed coral trout fillet on shaved abalone. Dining options range from good-value fixed-price lunches to the full tasting-menu delight.

Prime

GPO, 1 Martin Place; tel: 02 9229 7777; www.gposydney.com.au; Mon–Fri L, D, Sat D; $$$–$$$$

Above from far left: turf and surf; seafood is a speciality; refreshing dessert, just right for the hot summer.

When only meat will do, head for Prime. Nestled amid the sandstone arches in the basement of the historic GPO, the feel is gentleman's club, and the menu is aimed at carnivorous connoisseurs, detailing not just cuts but also breeds and ageing details. A treat for beefy boys and Wagyu women.

Spice Temple

10 Bligh Street; tel: 02 8078 1888; www.rockpool.com.au; Mon–Fri L, D, Sat D; $$–$$$

Globally acclaimed chef Neil Perry has opened (and closed) a number of venues over the years. He kicked 2009 off with a bang, opening two new restaurants in his Bligh Street premises: the relaxed Rockpool Bar and Grill and, in the basement, the atmospheric Spice Temple. The cuisine here is Chinese food, but not as you know it: Perry revels in the hot and tangy flavours of lesser-known provinces such as Hunan, Jiangxi and Xinjiang. A real treat for those with adventurous tastes.

Steel Bar and Grill

60 Carrington Street; tel: 02 9299 9997; www.steelbarandgrill.com; Mon–Fri L, D, Sat D; $$

There's an airy terrace, a flash interior heavy on industrial chic (the loos are a must-visit), and good-looking staff. However, they are not the only reasons that Steel is packed out at lunchtimes and after work. The food lives up to its surroundings and has something to appeal to every palate, from a Goan fish curry to salmon and steak.

Sushi-Choo

320 George Street; tel: 02 9240 3000; www.merivale.com.au; Mon–Fri L, D, Sat D; $–$$

Justin Hemmes's latest extravaganza, The Ivy, is home to a range of exceptionally cool restaurants, including an acclaimed steakhouse, but it is Sushi-Choo that is packing in Sydney's sushi fans. Two giant sushi trains carry an assortment of treats, while à la carte offerings include smoky beef *tataki* dressed with ginger and soy.

Tetsuya's

529 Kent Street; tel: 02 9267 2900; www.tetsuyas.com; Tue–Fri D, Sat L–D; $$$$

If you are serious about your food, you cannot leave town with eating at Tetsuya's. And if you are eating at Tet's, you can't not have the 12-course *dégustation* – because it is the only thing on the menu. The combination of Japanese and French influences makes each course an exquisite experience. Remember to book well in advance.

Opera House and Around

China Doll

6 Cowper Wharf Road, Woolloomooloo; tel: 02 9380 6744; www.chinadoll.com.au; daily L, D; $$$

Sydney offers a cornucopia of Asian foods, from Thai to Laotian, Korean to Vietnamese. If you cannot decide which one you feel like tonight, head for China Doll, where the menu reflects influences from all over the continent. Dishes such as tea-smoked ocean trout, and a prime location on the Finger Wharf, draw in the crowds despite the hefty prices.

Guillaume at Bennelong

Sydney Opera House, Bennelong Point; tel: 02 9241 1999; www. guillaumeatbennelong.com.au; Thur–Fri L, Mon–Sat D; $$$$

Almost every visitor to Sydney stops to marvel at the Opera House's shining exterior; only ticket-holders or the fortunate few who dine at Guillaume get to admire the structural interior, which is almost as elegant as the outside. Diners also get to savour some of the best French-influenced food in town. If your budget will not stretch that far, settle for post-theatre tapas in the upstairs bar.

Darling Harbour and Around

Golden Century

393–9 Sussex Street, Chinatown; tel: 02 9212 3901; www.golden century.com.au; daily L, D; $–$$

This is Chinatown at its most authentic: a vast 600-seater restaurant that is packed all hours of the day and late into the night, complete with gold wallpaper, a menu the size of an airport novel, and waiters carrying still-flapping seafood fresh from the tank. People either love it or hate it. Daily specials tend to offer more adventurous choices, while the less daring can stick with favourites like hotpot or crispy-skinned chicken.

The Malaya

King Street Wharf, 39 Lime Street; tel: 02 9279 1170; www.the malaya.com.au; Mon–Sat L, D, Sun D; $$

Well into its fourth decade, this old favourite has had a makeover, moving into a glamorous new home. Fortunately, although the decor has changed, the food has not. The Malaya still dishes up a broad range of Malaysian favourites, with the emphasis on the *nonya* cuisine of the country's Chinese community. If you love flavours of lemongrass, chilli, coconut and tamarind, this is the place for you.

Potts Point and Around
Cafe Sopra

81 Macleay Street, Potts Point; tel: 1300 552 119; www.fratellifresh. com.au; daily L, D; $$

Dining surrounded by boxes of leeks or large tins of olive oil may not be everyone's taste, but there's a reason that Fratelli Fresh – a provedore with its own inhouse restaurant, Cafe Sopra – is always packed, and that's the mouthwatering menu of rustic,

reasonably-priced Italian dishes made from the best seasonal produce.

Fratelli Paradiso

12 Challis Avenue, Potts Point; tel: 02 9357 1744; www.fratelliparadiso. com; Mon–Fri B, L, D, Sat–Sun B, L; $$

Challis Avenue is the heart of Potts Point's cafe society, lined with intimate eateries of every description. Whether Sunday brunch or Thursday night dinner, Fratelli Paradiso always has a couple of locals queued outside. They succeed by keeping it simple, offering a small selection of creatively updated Italian classics, including a couple of homemade pasta dishes.

Gazebo Wine Garden

2 Elizabeth Bay Road, Elizabeth Bay; tel: 02 9357 5333; www.the gazebos.com.au; Fri–Sun L, D, Mon–Thur D; $$

There is nothing one-dimensional about the Gazebo. Indoor-outdoor, wine bar-restaurant, classy-quirky (yes, that is a stuffed fox hanging from the ceiling), it is a great place to drop by

at any time of the day or well into the night. The friendly staff will happily help you choose a drop from the impressive wine list to wash down the classic bistro fare.

Darlinghurst and Surry Hills

Bodega

216 Commonwealth Street, Surry Hills; tel: 02 9212 7766; www.bodegatapas.com; Thur–Fri L, D, Mon–Wed and Sat D; $$–$$$

Bodega offers the complete package: funky surroundings, gorgeous waiters, and an inviting tapas menu that makes it hard to say 'enough'. Their take on fish fingers – sashimi kingfish on garlic toast with cuttlefish and *mojama* – is a perfect blend of contrasting textures, while more daring combinations, such as seared scallops with pickled Wagyu tongue, also delight. The house tortilla remains the *pièce de résistance*.

Fish Face

132 Darlinghurst Road, Darlinghurst; tel: 02 9332 4803; www.fishface. com.au; Mon–Sat D; $$

Before Sydneysiders fell for sushi, they were addicted to fish and chips. At Fish Face, you can have either. One of Sydney's best seafood restaurants is a tiny diner nestled into a narrow space on an inner-city street far from the sea. With super-fresh produce, unfussy presentation and a buzzing vibe, Fish Face proves that small can be beautiful.

Above from far left: fish and chips, Sydney-style; all set for a stylish dinner.

Price for a two-course meal for one person with a glass of house wine:	
$$$$	over A$90
$$$	A$70–90
$$	A$50–70
$	below A$50

Longrain

85 Commonwealth Street,
Surry Hills; tel: 02 9280 2888;
www.longrain.com.au; Wed–Fri,
Sun, L, daily D; $$$

Sydney's glam crowd flocks to this converted 100-year-old warehouse both for its chic bar with some of the best cocktails in town, and for the adjoining restaurant that turns Thai food into high art. Do not let the communal tables fool you: prices are far from cheap, but dishes such as grilled veal ribs with coconut sauce and hot sour salad are worth it.

Mohr Fish

202 Devonshire Street, Surry Hills;
tel: 02 9318 1326; daily L, D; $–$$

As this tiny, unpretentious fish and chippie doesn't take bookings, most patrons end up nursing a beer in the pub next door while waiting for a table to clear. The wait is worth it. The menu sticks to simple fish dishes, but the fish selection is fantastic and beautifully cooked, while entrees range from fish dumplings to mussel bouillabaisse.

Souk in the City

Shop 5, 431 Bourke Street, Surry
Hills; tel: 02 9357 7577; www.souk
inthecity.com; Tue–Sun D; $$–$$$

For sheer entertainment value, it's hard to go past this Moroccan-inspired diner. You may be showered with rose petals on arrival; you'll certainly enjoy soaking up the atmospheric lantern-lit, cushion-strewn interiors, the fabulous cocktails, and delicious morsels such as the pigeon pie.

Una's

338–40 Victoria Street, Darlinghurst;
tel: 02 9360 6885;
www.unas.com.au; daily B, L, D; $

The hip Victoria Street strip is perhaps the last place you would expect to find an old-fashioned Austrian diner, but Una's has held onto its prime position for more than three decades, making it older than many of its clientele. Una's is famous for serving up huge portions of hearty fare, whether it's a laden breakfast platter or a plate of veal schnitzel that still gets you change from a twenty.

Universal

Republic 2, Palmer Street, Darlinghurst; tel: 02 9331 0709;
www.universalrestaurant.com;
Mon–Sat D; $$–$$$

Christine Manfield, one of Sydney's most acclaimed chefs, takes her inspiration from all around the globe, delivering a melting pot of flavour-packed morsels. Her 'tasting portions' are sized somewhere between an entree and a main; order several to share to get the full effect. Each dish is matched with a wine by the glass, often sourced from smaller, lesser-known vineyards. A feast for the senses.

Victoria Room

Level 1, 235 Victoria Street, Darling-hurst; tel: 02 9357 4488; www.the victoriaroom.com; Tue–Sun D; $$

When we say The Victoria Room has an identity crisis, we mean it in the nicest possible way. The decor of the loft-style space has a Casablanca feel, with palm trees, banquettes, fringed table lamps and decorative screens. The food, on the other hand, sits between the Mediterranean and the Middle East. The bar attracts young funksters, while on weekend afternoons, an indulgent high tea is served.

North Bondi Italian

118–20 Ramsgate Avenue, North Bondi; tel: 02 9300 4400; www.idrb.com; Wed–Sun L, D, Mon–Tue D; $$–$$$

In some ways, this restaurant is quintessential Bondi. It has the beachside location and the hip factor, evident in everything from the chic dining room and the good-looking staff to the throng of gorgeous young things who seem to be perpetually waiting for a table (there's a no-bookings policy). What may come as a surprise, however, is the menu, which skips the pizza and pastas for inspired Italian cuisine.

Pompei's

126–30 Roscoe Street, Bondi Beach; tel: 02 9365 1233; www.pompeis.com.au; Fri–Sun L, D, Tue–Thur D; $–$$

If you are desperate for dinner at 6pm, you may need to find somewhere else as it is rush hour at this family-friendly joint, with children and prams tucked into every cranny. At other times though, Pompei's offers quality Italian a block from the beach. Thin-crust pizza, homemade pasta and fruity sorbets are deserved favourites.

Sean's Panaroma

270 Campbell Parade, Bondi Beach; tel: 02 9365 4924; www.seans panaroma.com.au; Wed–Fri D, Sat L, D, Sun L; $$$

Sean Moran likes to do things his way. His opening hours prove that, unlike most chefs, he appreciates having a life, another reason, perhaps, why he has stayed in the same location for years. Although his food could easily grace some of the city's most acclaimed dining rooms, he has stuck with this cosy beachside canteen, and his clientele love him for it.

Above from far left: expert glass-handling; traditional decor at the Victoria Room; clean, contemporary lines at Universal.

Price for a two-course meal for one person with a glass of house wine:

$$$$	over A$80
$$$	A$60–80
$$	A$40–60
$	below A$40

There is no real arts precinct in Sydney, although the Sydney Theatre Company's two theatres have turned Walsh Bay into a fledgling hub. From converted stables in Kings Cross to reconfigured carriage halls in the inner west, a range of venues is scattered throughout the city. This is by no means an exhaustive list, but does include the major venues for each art form.

Theatre

Belvoir Street Theatre

25 Belvoir Street, Surry Hills; tel: 02 9699 3444; www.belvoir.com.au

Geoffrey Rush and Cate Blanchett are just two of the actors who made their names with Company B, the talented troupe assembled by Neil Armfield, one of Australian theatre's great talents. The repertoire ranges from classic to new international hits and fresh local talent. The Upstairs Theatre seats 350, while the intimate 80-seater Downstairs space hosts fringe productions.

The Stables

10 Nimrod Street, Kings Cross; tel: 9332 1052; www.griffintheatre. com.au

This tiny theatre located in a former stables in the backstreets of Kings Cross is home to the Griffin Theatre Company, which has a reputation for breaking fresh young talent. Mondays are pay-what-you-can nights (minimum A$10).

The Wharf

Pier 4 and 5 Hickson Road, Walsh Bay; tel: 02 9250 1777; www.sydneytheatre.com.au

The Sydney Theatre Company (STC) has not just a high-wattage power couple at the helm (Cate Blanchett and her playwright husband, Andrew Upton), but also a stunning home in an atmospheric converted wharf. The STC's typically crowd-pleasing roster has got a bit adventurous of late, with international performers such as Liv Ullman and Philip Seymour Hoffman popping in to direct. Their second venue, the Sydney Theatre (22 Hickson Road, Walsh Bay; tel: 9250 1999; www.sydneytheatre.org.au), is across the road from The Wharf.

Dance

Carriageworks

245 Wilson Street, Eveleigh; tel: 02 8571 9099; www.carriageworks. com.au

This beautifully converted train repair yard is one of Sydney's newest venues. It hosts performances from the Sydney Dance Company, the indigenous Bangarra Dance Theatre, and visiting troupes. Fans of industrial architecture will love its interior; the performers love the expansive, adaptable stage.

Classical Music

City Recital Hall

Angel Place; tel: 02 8256 2222; www.cityrecitalhall.com

This low-key venue in the heart of the CBD regularly hosts performances from Australia's most acclaimed classical ensembles, including the Brandenburg Orchestra. Particularly worth catching are performances by the Australian Chamber Orchestra, known for its varied programme of classics and new commissions, and for the A$10 million Del Gesù antique violin, rumoured to have once belonged to Paganini, played by orchestra leader, Richard Tognetti.

Sydney Opera House

Bennelong Point; tel: 02 9250 7777; www.sydneyoperahouse.com

Do not let the name fool you; there is more than classical music on offer at the Opera House. It is home to several of Australia's flagship performing arts companies, including Opera Australia and the Sydney Symphony Orchestra, and is the Sydney venue for the Melbourne-based Australian Ballet. In addition, the Drama Theatre and the Playhouse focus on mainstream theatre, including productions by Bell Shakespeare, Australia's only theatre company dedicated to the Bard. The intimate Studio offers a range of cutting-edge local and overseas dramatic and musical productions.

Jazz

The Basement

7 Macquarie Place, Circular Quay; tel: 02 9251 2797; www.the basement.com.au

For decades Sydney's premier jazz and blues venue, The Basement has hosted all the big names, including Dizzy Gillespie, Herbie Hancock and Prince. World music, pop and alternative acts also make appearances at this wonderfully intimate venue. Early birds can book a table for dinner, guaranteeing you the best seats in the house.

Woollahra Hotel

116 Queen Street, Woollahra; tel: 02 9327 9777; www.woollahra hotel.com.au

This sleek eastern-suburbs watering hole has live jazz on Sunday nights, and Sydney's best world music on Thursday nights, with everything from Brazilian funk to Afro-Cuban jazz. Once you have worked up an appetite on the dance floor, enjoy a Wagyu beef burger upstairs in the Moncur Terrace bistro.

Rock and Pop/ Contemporary Music

Enmore Theatre

118–132 Enmore Road, Newtown; tel: 02 9550 3666; www.enmore theatre.com.au

Generations of Sydneysiders have watched their favourite bands grind it out on the stage of the Art Deco Enmore Theatre, Sydney's oldest running live music venue. From international headliners to local faves, they all play here. The building's faded glory is part of its charm, and the acoustics are excellent.

Above from far left: Cate Blanchett and Andrew Upton launching the 2011 Main Stage Season for the Sydney Theatre Company; the Klaxons performing at the Enmore Theatre.

Metro Theatre

624 George Street; tel: 02 9550 3666; www.metrotheatre.com.au

Good old-fashioned rock venue in the heart of the CBD, with a pumping mosh pit and sticky floors. Lots of international bands play here, notably rock and hip-hop acts. Its central location makes it easy to catch a taxi home.

Oxford Art Factory

38–46 Oxford Street, Darlinghurst; tel: 02 9332 3711; www.oxfordart factory.com

In the past couple of years, the Oxford Art Factory has established itself as a hub for all kinds of art. In addition to the exhibitions on the walls, the Live Art Space hosts international and local performers from genres ranging from rock and pop to burlesques and cabaret. The bar is a cool place to chill out.

Film

Dendy Opera Quays

Shop 9, 2 East Circular Quay; tel: 02 9247 3800; www.dendy.com.au

Dendy Films is Australia's premier art-house chain, and this is the jewel in their crown, perched on the edge of Sydney's foreshore. The best of local and foreign arthouse films are screened here and you can enjoy a glass of wine with your film.

The Verona

17 Oxford Street, Paddington; tel: 02 9360 6099; www.palace cinemas.com.au

Another favourite with the arthouse crowd, The Verona wins points for its Oxford Street location, which makes it easy to grab a bite after the show. Its major drawback is the box office on the pavement, which makes queuing for popular sessions a drag. Get your tickets early, then browse through the excellent Ariel bookshop opposite.

Bars and Clubs

Arthouse Hotel

275 Pitt Street; tel: 02 9284 1200; www.thearthousehotel.com.au

This is a centrally located venue in a heritage building that has something for everyone. Urban sophisticates head upstairs for the stunning 19th-century architecture, the sleek design and the refined vibe. Huge raves downstairs on Friday and Saturday nights attract a younger crowd. Decent restaurant too.

Blu Bar

Shangri-La Hotel, 176 Cumberland Street; tel: 02 9250 6013

Not content with offering possibly the best view in Sydney, Blu Horizon also has a great cocktail list. Take the express lift to the top, where you will be dazzled by the stellar harbour view from floor-to-ceiling windows.

The Ivy Bar

330 George Street; tel: 02 9240 3000; www.merivale.com.au

Justin Hemmes is Sydney's king of cool, the man behind some of the city's

best-loved pleasure palaces, including Establishment and Slip Inn, where a Danish prince met his Australian princess. The Ivy is his latest venture and its centrepiece is The Ivy Bar, a sleek space where you can pose at the bar, curl up in a corner, or simply dance the night away, as long as you are cool enough to get past the door staff.

The Piano Room

Corner of Kings Cross and Darlinghurst roads; tel: 02 8324 4500; www.pianoroom.com.au

Nestled under the Coke sign (the entrance is on Kings Cross Road), The Piano Room is a laidback playground that has been an instant hit with grown-up types who like dim lighting, music that does not drown out all conversation, and a central location. Relaxed yet swinging most nights of the week.

Time To Vino

Ground floor, Diamant Hotel, 141 Kings Cross Road, Potts Point; tel: 02 9380 4252; www.timetovino.com

For years, Sydney lagged behind Melbourne in the groovy wine bar stakes, but over the last few years a spate of new openings has started to redress the balance. Time to Vino is known for its superb wine list and its friendly and chic vibe.

Above from far left: DJ P-Money (left) and Vince Harder perform live on stage during MTV's The Lair at the Metro Theatre; Blu Horizon bar.

Gay and Lesbian Venues

Oxford Street is the epicentre of gay Sydney, with a range of venues catering for all tastes. Hotspots include the super-sleek Slide (41 Oxford Street, Darlinghurst; tel: 02 8915 1899; Wed–Sun until late), housed in a former bank and offering a dining and cabaret show as well as a buzzing dance floor. Old favourites include the welcoming Colombian Hotel (corner Oxford and Crown streets, Darlinghurst; tel: 02 9360 2151; www.colombian.com.au; Mon–Fri 9am–6am, Sat–Sun 11am–6am) and Midnight Shift (85 Oxford Street, Darlinghurst; tel: 02 9360 4319; www.themidnightshift.com; daily until late): the drag shows upstairs are well worth the price of admission, while there's no cover charge at the downstairs bar. If your idea of a good time is dancing the night away, try the pumping Arq (16 Flinders Street, Taylor Square; tel: 02 9380 8700; www.arqsydney.com.au; open from Fri 11pm to Mon 6am). Away from Oxford Street, venues include Newtown's Bank Hotel (324 King Street; tel: 02 8568 1900; www.bankhotel.com.au; open 7 nights until late), where punters have the choice between moody interiors or a multi-level beer garden. Wednesdays are dyke night; another popular lesbian venue nearby is The Sly Fox (199 Enmore Road, Enmore; tel: 02 9557 1016; Wed–Sun; open from 10am until late).

CREDITS

Insight Step by Step Sydney
Written by: Ute Junker, John Borthwick
and David McGonigal
Series Editor: Sarah Sweeney
Cartography Editor: Zoë Goodwin
Cartographic Production:
Phoenix Mapping Ltd
Picture Manager: Steven Lawrence

Photography: All photography by APA/Glyn
Genin and Jon Davison except:
Alamy 68, 75-1, 75-2, 90-2; Amora Hotel 108;
Axiom 8-5, 60-2, 62-1, 63; Botanic Gardens
Trust/Simone Cottrell 2-2; Botanic Gardens
Trust/ Jaime Plaza 39, 90-1; Chelsea Hotel 112-
2; City Recital Hall 94-3; Sergio Dionisio/Getty
Images 122; John Fotiadis/ Newspix/Rex Features
120–121; Fotolibra 2-1, 8-2; Getty Images 48,
58-3, 61-1, 121; Courtesy Golden Century 14-3
Guillaume at Bennelong 8-6; Heidrun Lohr 20;
Hilton Hotel 94-2; 109; Hotel Altamont 94-7,
112-1, 113; iStockphoto.com 4-1, 4-4, 10-2, 11-
2, 13-1, 15-2, 16-2, 22-1, 23-2, 26-4, 41-2, 42-1,
42-2, 44-2, 45-1. 45-2, 53, 66-1, 71-1, 84-1, 84-
2, 84-4, 85-1, 86, 87, 89, 93-1, 94-1, 97, 98–99,
106–107; Longrain 94-4, 94-5, 94-6, 117; Mary
Evans 25; Photolibrary 2-7, 76, 77, 91; Rex Features 55-2, 120; Scala Archive 24; Scenic World
8-4, 8-7, 88-1; Shangri La Hotel 110, 123;
Sydney Wildlife World 84-3; Topfoto 7-2, 74;
Tourism Australia 8-1, 26-2, 30, 72-1, 73-1;
Tourism New South Wales 7-1-3, 10-1, 13-3, 22-
2, 26-6, 60-1, 66-2, 79, 81, 82, 83, 88-2, 92-2;
Universal 119; Victoria Room 118-2; Vulcan
Hotel 111

Front cover: main image - photolibrary.com;
small front images - iStockhoto.com;
back cover images - fotolia.co.uk

Printed by: CTPS-China

©2011 Apa Publications (UK) Limited
All rights reserved
Second Edition 2011

No part of this book may be reproduced, stored
in a retrieval system or transmitted in any form
or by any means (electronic, mechanical, photo-
copying, recording or otherwise), without prior
written permission of APA Publications. Brief text
quotations with use of photographs are exempted
for book review purposes only. Information has
been obtained from sources believed to be reli-
able, but its accuracy and completeness, and the
opinions based thereon, are not guaranteed.

Although Insight Guides and the authors of this
book have taken all reasonable care in preparing it,
we make no warranty about the accuracy or completeness of its content, and, to the maximum extent
permitted, disclaim all liability arising from its use.

CONTACTING THE EDITORS

We would appreciate it if readers would alert us
to errors or outdated information by writing to
us at insight@apaguide.co.uk or APA Publications,
PO Box 7910, London SE1 1WE, UK.

www.insightguides.com

DISTRIBUTION

Worldwide

**APA Publications GmbH & Co. Verlag KG
(Singapore branch)**
7030 Ang Mo Kio Ave 5
08-65 Northstar @ AMK, Singapore 569880
Email: apasin@singnet.com.sg

UK and Ireland

GeoCenter International Ltd
Meridian House, Churchill Way West
Basingstoke, Hampshire RG21 6YR
Email: sales@geocenter.co.uk

US

Ingram Publisher Services
One Ingram Blvd, PO Box 3006
La Vergne, TN 37086-1986
Email: customer.service@ingrampublisher
services.com

Australia

Universal Publishers
PO Box 307
St. Leonards NSW 1590
Email: sales@universalpublishers.com.au

INDEX